SADDLE SORE SPIRITUALITY

Bike to the Bible

A beginners guide to the wonderful world of cycling

By
Bob Blaylock

Copyright © 2012 by Bob Blaylock

SADDLE SORE SPIRITUALITY
by Bob Blaylock

Printed in the United States of America

ISBN 9781624197338

All rights reserved solely by the author. The author guarantees all contents are original and do not infringe upon the legal rights of any other person or work. No part of this book may be reproduced in any form without the permission of the author. The views expressed in this book are not necessarily those of the publisher.

Unless otherwise indicated, Bible quotations are taken from the King James Version.

www.xulonpress.com

Table of Contents

Introduction vii

Chapter 1. Only Believe 15

Chapter 2. In the Beginning......................... 28

Chapter 3. Keep the Load Easy 48

Chapter 4. A Proper Way to Do Everything..... 62

Chapter 5. Keep Your Eyes Upon Jesus 81

Chapter 6. Captains and Seamen................ 100

Chapter 7. The Off Season 124

Chapter 8. Say It Ain't So........................... 138

Chapter 9. Proper Etiquette Please.............. 174

Chapter 10. The Ultimate Commitment........ 198

Chapter 11. Ride Like a Champion today 217

Chapter 12. It's Not About the Bike............. 244

Glossary of Biking Terms........................... 255

INTRODUCTION

I began cycling seriously in 1978 more as a matter of economics than recreation. We were a young Navy family and owned a '72 Oldsmobile Cutlass that, at best, was about as fuel efficient as a Freightliner truck. I was stationed at the Naval Construction Battalion Center on the Mississippi Gulf Coast and we lived about four miles from the base. So, with a reasonable commute distance, year-around warm weather, and a Second Class Petty Officer's meager paycheck a bicycle was a great alternative to the stately Olds.

My family will attest to my frugality. I think of it more as efficient shopping: very efficient shopping. You know, God expects us to be good stewards. Whatever the motive, I shopped for days for the best buy in a bike. Now, I was less than a novice and had not a clue what to look for in a bicycle except for price. My young son, Michael, and I trailed to every discount store on the Gulf Coast, twice and more, until I decided on an $89 no-name, 26-inch, fat-tire ten-speed. I have just spent more than that on tires for my most recent ride.

That blue ten-speed was my pride and joy. It served me well for a couple of years as "Trigger" (Named after Roy Rogers faithful steed) and I learned the basics of cycling on that sturdy old bike. I discovered the Gulf Coast on that bike and explored the west of Spain from her saddle. I discovered cycling in those few months with "Trigger."

Now, an estimated 150,000 miles and eight bikes later, I am still riding and loving it. God has blessed me with a wonderful avocation, recreation, and lifestyle. I have ridden in more foreign countries than most people even dream of visiting. I have raced. Well, I have *participated* in races. I have toured the most beautiful places in this world. My bike has been my prescription that has enabled me to deal with my diabetes. It has kept me young in spirit, healthy and happy for many years and hopefully many years to come. I plan to continue riding until Jesus comes. In short, I love cycling. It keeps me fit and young. It has been wonderful therapy both physically and emotionally. It keeps me humble. It affords lots of time and opportunity to appreciate God's wonders and it gives me the solitude to hear Him speak to me.

INTRODUCTION

Since I frequently ride alone and on quiet country roads, I have a great opportunity to talk to and listen to the Lord: to pray often on the bike. Some of that prayer is peaceful; some is more urgent and aggressive, depending on conditions like traffic and terrain. Some are prayers of thanks: again, many times depending on traffic or terrain. Some are prayers for forgiveness depending on motorists, dogs, and occasionally other cyclists. I enjoy those long, solitary rides where I can ask God questions and I have the time to hear his answers. We talk. Many times I just listen.

I have gained fitness, skill, experience, and knowledge over the years and miles. My bikes have gone everywhere with me. I was assigned to a ten-month deployment to Spain and "Trigger" went with me. Trigger and I were able to experience Spain in a way none of my Navy shipmates could. I still have memories that make me smile when I reminisce all alone. My bikes went with me on shipboard and on other assignments where I was able to ride during port calls and experience France, Spain, Italy and other parts of the world like no other visitor can.

Now, I need to explain that I am not an *expert* cyclist. That is a disclaimer I learned from testifying in legal hearings in relation to my assignments as an evidence photographer. I was a twenty-five year career Navy Photographers Mate, and I continue my photo profession with a part-time photographic business. I was coached to *never* claim to be an expert but cite my experience and training as credentials. An expert should have all the correct answers to any question relating to his or her profession. Even an inept lawyer can trip up a self-proclaimed "expert." I do have a great deal of cycling experience and knowledge. As I used to tell the young sailors under my charge, I may not have all the answers, but I certainly have made all the mistakes. I can tell you what *not* to do. So, as you read this book, understand that I speak more from lessons of error than from the podium of a professor.

The assignment to write *Saddle Sore Spirituality* came to me while on a lonesome fifty-mile ride on a calm Sunday afternoon shortly after I had completed my sixth 150-mile Tour De Cure charity ride for the American Diabetes Association. I was having a wonderful, slow, and relaxing ride when God spoke to me and told me to write a book about cycling. He was very specific. Don't you hate it when He does that? I was to write about my experiences on the bike and to compare the skills and truths associated with cycling to the truths needed to "travel" on life's spiritual journey.

INTRODUCTION

My first reaction was, I imagine, much like Moses' when God spoke to him. Moses argued that he was not a leader, public speaker, young, etc, etc, etc. I reminded God that I am not an "expert" cyclist and certainly I'm not a skilled writer: much less an author. "I have no experience at this." There was a very long and silent pause while I glided along the country road. I broke the silence and respectfully asked out loud, "ME?" Well, except for a few cows and the occasional squirrel, it was God and me on that road in Wilson County Tennessee. Of course He was talking to me. The answer was, as you may have guessed, a simple "Yes!"

"But I can't write."

God reminded me that I had recently written a short story about my struggle up Monteagle Mountain on the Tour De Cure that year and everyone who read it loved it.

"Oh yes, You **would** bring that up."

"But, I'm just an avid rider, certainly not someone who can write as an expert with authority on cycling."

Long pause. God: "I will guide you." Very long pause. "Did you think Noah was a salty ol' sea captain before the flood? He did okay"

"But, I'm not a Bible scholar. What about that?" Now I had Him!

"I will teach you." No good answer to that is there?

As I rode, He put in my thoughts some wonderful examples of the parallels between cycling truths and His truths. Boy it sounded like a good idea. So, right there on Chicken Road (yes, there is a Chicken Road in rural Wilson County, Tennessee) I simply said "yes."

He showed me simple parallels to write about. The very concept—the physics—that allows a two wheel, rather top-heavy machine to stay upright is evidence of the bewildering power of our God. And, the old cliché that says, "It's like riding a bike, you never forget how" has spiritual parallels. Once we discover God's truths, we can depend on them for eternity. He reminded me that learning to ride as a child is easier than mastering the bike as an adult, and if we bring up a child in the ways of the Lord he will never depart from them. God has told us to come to Him as little children. Wonder why?

Saddle Sore Spirituality I hope will inspire some of you to get on a bike and experience some of the wonders of cycling that have blessed me. Maybe some of you will gain insight into the sport and be able to enjoy it as a spectator. You see, I believe that God wants us to "have life and have it more abundantly," and I believe He has given us cycling

INTRODUCTION

for our pleasure and health: "...life more abundantly." But, whether you ever put foot to pedal, or whether you ever follow the Tour De France in July, let God talk to you and teach you His truths so that you may grow in faith and knowledge in your journey through your spiritual life. God has so many things to teach all of us I pray that whatever your motive in reading this book you will allow God to talk to you and to grow you in His wonderful gifts that he has in store for you.

Chapter 1

ONLY BELIEVE

The wonder of the bicycle has amazed me ever since I was a young boy. I've thought about it often. My being not very athletic and a little coordination challenged has only enhanced my curiosity. As a child, falling down was an accepted part of my life. But, at the tender age of six or seven I was able to manage to stay upright on a bicycle. Amazing!

How does it work? It's a mystery. It was a mystery then and it remains a mystery now. I've often thought it similar to the enigma of how helicopters fly? I'm told helicopters and bumblebees aren't supposed to be able fly. They defy the basic laws of physics. So how can they exist? They work, I'm convinced, by sheer determination. They simply pour on enough power, effort, and resolve to beat the air to exhaustion and gravity into submission. Now, I can understand that. Apply enough power and tenacity and things can overcome even gravity.

The bicycle on the other hand actually works with very little apparent gusto. A couple turns of the pedal and you're there; gliding down the road, wind in your face, free from all worries. We don't see a great deal of brute power there. A bicycle is an entirely different concept to the muscle and tenacity theory used by helicopters and bumblebees. No matter how much power a person puts into "forcing" a bicycle to stand upright, it just does not succumb to the demand. Ever walk away from your bike and forget to lean it against something? You can't *force* it to balance itself. It has no power of its own to defy gravity.

When the Scotsman Kirkpatrick MacMillan (Uncle Angus) invented the pedal powered bicycle back in 1839 he must have had an extra, double portion of faith; or, more likely, an extra, double portion of Scotch whisky. How could he have imagined that a machine would balance itself on two, skinny wheels and then transport a 10 stone man down the glen? It is, by design, destined to fall over. Bob's seat-of-the-pants-science law number 1 tells us the obvious: that things don't balance very well on two points. Three works, but two is a problem. And, Bob's science law number

2 observes that things heavier on the top than the bottom tend to fall over unless held up by some sort of support. These simple laws alone should tell us that the two-wheeler won't work. But, we add to the difficulty by making one of the wheels unstable: turnable. You know, that's the one in front that makes it steer. Now we have a contraption that is top-heavy *and* unstable. Sounds like a ready-made formula for failure to me.

Okay Uncle Angus now puts a man on top of this contraption to make it really top-heavy. The top now weighs something like ten times the bottom. Logically that's backwards.

If the bike were to be invented today I wonder if the whole idea would be thrown out during the first Engineering Project Committee meeting? I can hear it now. "Angus, this won't work. The stupid thing falls over on its own. Let's make a four-wheeler."

As if old Angus didn't have enough trouble falling down all by himself on his way home from the pub, he added up all these design features and then thought, "I'll make at speed dooooon the rhoooad as well. Just wait ta youuu see this." What was he thinking? As if simply falling down would not cause enough injury, he added forward motion and speed. Knee and elbow pads were not to be invented for several more decades. The town doctor must have been well pleased. With Angus's new folly and all the business it would bring in, ole Doctor McDouglas might be getting a new horse and buggy or maybe even opening another practice: a Cyclist-Nut clinic.

Think about it. We have a machine with all the physical design features to make it fall over, but it doesn't. How can that be? Oh, I know that physics gives us all the pointy-headed laws and formulas that prove the concept of bodies in motion... and inertia... and.... All they have done is *observe* that something works and make up some big-worded rules that support that observation. I can do that! I have observed every time I ride up a mountain I slow down. Therefore, Bob's Law of Mountains states that: mountains exert a negative force on all bicycles. *And*: The bigger the mountain the greater the negative force. Okay? That's my scientific law. It happens *every time*. It's my law, but it still does not explain the *why* part. It happens, but why? Or, how about this one: I observe that every time I try to show off on a group ride, some twenty-something-year-old skinny so-and-so goes off the front and drops me like a bad habit. ...Happens every time. Everyone knows it happens, so it must be some great law.

The bottom line is that I, and I'll bet most of you; really don't comprehend why a bicycle works.

How on earth, just because a wheel is spinning, can an unstable, top-heavy machine with very simplistic construction stay upright? Yes, I know all the academic masterminds quote all the rules, but why do those rules exist? It's still a mystery. I'm starting to sound like a child repeatedly asking "Why?" But, why? As many miles and hours as I have ridden over the years, occasionally I still whisper to myself, "How? How can this work?" Do you ever *really* wonder? I mean, let's face it, the whole concept that simply by rolling the wheel, an otherwise unstable mass of metal will glide down the road with grace and sureness is mind-boggling. It just does not make sense. But, it works!

I can almost buy into the science of *bodies in motion tend to stay in motion* and justify that the wheels with their rotating mass tend to keep the whole thing stable. Then I tilt my head a little and question how a 700-gram wheel can possibly keep a forty-pound bike upright and moving. In the battle of moving masses, the forty-pounder part wins hands down. Okay, okay; keep the wheel moving fast enough and even a little weight on a flywheel-like object will exert a great effect. Yes, but.... Yes, but the bike still works its wonder even at a dawdling pace. Track racing cyclists can creep around a banked oval at no more than a snail's pace even stopping on top of the bank for long periods of time waiting for the other guy to make his move. I've tried that. Believe me, it's not easy. I made a quick decision to be a road-racing guy, not a track racer. But, it does work.

I have also experienced riding steep climbs and mountains with all the strength I can muster and being pleased to maintain any forward (and upward) motion. I have been on climbs where I could only manage two or maybe three miles per hour while thrashing side to side in a mad attempt to put every microgram of power to the pedals while gasping for any air my lungs could process. Know what? The bike stayed upright and served me like a trusted old horse out of the old west. It just ain't supposed to work.

Yes, I know, the human phenomenon and the miracle of balance may play an important role in the feasibility of the bicycle. Tightrope walkers and high-rise construction workers do exist. But, not every kid in the world is an acrobat or a steel-beam-walker. Kids learn to ride bikes at about the peak of the clumsiness lifecycle. It's as if they already have that ability built into their being; they just don't know it. Give a kid fifteen minutes on top of a Schwinn and he rides for the rest of his life. I remember my grandfather, well into his seventies, having not been on a bike in probably fifty years and suffering terribly from Parkinson's disease climbed on my old, red Columbia and took off like he was a ten-year-old. Amazing! I used play darts almost daily. If I don't throw for a few weeks we are remodeling the wall behind the dartboard. If tennis players don't play for a while they have to regain the skills to compete. Don't get near a golfer who has been off the links for a year or more. In almost any other activity the rule of "use it or lose it" applies. Not cycling. Oh you may be winded for a few rides, but ride you can. The skills to stay upright, pedal, and steer **never** leave you.

Brilliant minds in human history have called the bicycle one of the most important and astounding inventions of all time. It may be one of the simplest of machines ever invented but yet an utterly astonishing thing. It is the primary mode of transportation in most underdeveloped countries. Underdeveloped?

After the massive California earthquakes a few years ago, transportation was nonexistent and communication was terribly restricted. People on mountain bikes, however, were able to transit Los Angeles and San Francisco with ease bringing much-needed medical supplies to the hardest hit areas and becoming, in some cases, the only means of getting messages in and out of devastated areas. Police departments worldwide are mobilizing officers on bicycles and discovering that bike-patrols are perhaps the most efficient method of law enforcement available to congested cities. They are quick when necessary. They are completely maneuverable. They allow the officer the personal, face-to-face contact with the citizens they are protecting that is impossible with a squad car and as effective as an officer on foot patrol. Police are beginning to get to know the people in the neighborhoods again, and the people are getting to know and to trust the cop on the beat. Crime is down, and trust in the police is up. Donut shops are being boarded up.

During the oil shortage and gasoline crisis of the mid-seventies the bicycle became the only viable alternative transportation for many Americans. In fact, it is speculated that the oil dilemma actually saved a floundering and perhaps dying bicycle industry. As gasoline prices again reach record highs I wonder if the bike will enjoy a second resurgence.

So, we have a phenomenon: the bicycle. It's something that has touched nearly every life in recent history. It is an amazing, unexplainable thing that rarely fails us. It is the same for all. The basic design is the same whether it is a twenty-speed road bike, a rough and tumble mountain bike, a neighborhood cruiser, or a track racer. How much we depend on the bike and how much we benefit is entirely up to the desire of the individual. It can be the daily commuter, the freedom machine, the health saving device, the stress-escaper, the relax catalyst, and the list goes on and on. Yet, as much as it may be able to impact our lives from youth through old age, we still can't really explain how or why this thing works. It just does. Amazing!

"Believe in the Lord Jesus Christ and thou shalt be saved." I have another, more amazing, phenomenon in my life: the absolute power and the unyielding love of God. I cannot begin to explain Him or His might, or His love, or His gift of Jesus, or His plan for salvation, or His creation. I only know that HE is. Paul confirms this in his second letter to the Corinthians when he says, *"For we walk by faith, not by sight:"* 2 Corinthians 5:7. And, Jesus tells us in Matthew 19:26: **"But Jesus beheld them, and said unto them, With men this is impossible; but with God all things are possible."**

I cannot begin to explain how He spoke and creation happened. But I know it did. How do I know? I see His creation every day. I see it up close on every bike ride I take. *"By the word of the LORD were the heavens made; and all the host of them by the breath of his mouth.* [7] *He gathereth the waters of the sea together as an heap: he layeth up the depth in storehouses.⁸ Let all the earth fear the LORD: let all the inhabitants of the world stand in awe of him.⁹ For he spake, and it was done; he commanded, and it stood fast."* Psalms 33:6-9

I cannot comprehend how the love between a man and a woman can create an infant that is perfectly formed and simply by its very presence can bring so much pure joy to everyone around. But He can do that. How? Why? *"For thou hast possessed my reins: thou hast covered me in my mother's womb. ¹⁴ I will praise thee; for I am fearfully and wonderfully made: marvellous are thy works; and that my soul knoweth right well. ¹⁵ My substance was not hid from thee, when I was made in secret, and curiously wrought in the lowest parts of the earth. ¹⁶ Thine eyes did see my substance, yet being unperfect; and in thy book all my members were written, which in continuance were fashioned, when as yet there was none of them. ¹⁷ How precious also are thy thoughts unto me, O God! how great is the sum of them! ¹⁸ If I should count them, they are more in number than the sand: when I awake, I am still with thee."* Psalms 139:13

How can the most vile of offenders give their spirit and soul to God and be changed thoroughly and permanently into a loving and caring servant?

I do not know *how* He can; I humbly only know *that* He *can*. *"For God so loved the world, that He gave His only begotten son that **whosoever** believeth in Him should not perish, but have everlasting life.* John 3:16

How can a man be born of a virgin? Don't know. How does His death create life? Don't know. Just as I know that my seventeen-pound bicycle can carry me swiftly and safely for miles on end and that I can't explain why, I also know, without any doubt, that I have everlasting life in Him. Do I need to know how, why? No more than I need to know that I can sit on top of a contraption that should not work but I trust without thought that it will carry me safely to the mountain top and down again. It makes no difference if it climbs the mountain at three miles per hour or it descends around treacherous, blind curves at fifty miles per hour. I trust it because it has proven true over and over and over again. *"The Lord is my rock, and my fortress, and my deliverer; my God, my strength, in whom I will trust; my buckler, and the horn of my salvation, and my high tower."* Psalms 18:2,

"It's like riding a bike, you never forget how." Ever heard that axiom? It's true. Once you learn to ride, you are a changed person. You will always be able to ride. God's love, Jesus salvation, and the promise of everlasting life in Him is assured from acceptance of Jesus through eternity. Everlasting! You are a changed soul: FOREVER! Oh, if you stray away from Him for a time you may struggle for a while; but you remain His child through eternity. Let's have a new axiom: "It's like giving your life to Him, He never forgets you." *"For the Lord thy God is a merciful God; He will not forsake thee, neither destroy thee, nor forget the covenant of thy fathers which He sware unto them.* Deuteronomy 4:31. *"...for He hath said, I will never leave thee nor forsake thee."* Hebrews 13:5.

I need not ask the Lord how. His ways are not my ways. I need only to trust and obey. Many principles exist to fully employ the ability of the bicycle. If I tried to "understand" them I may not be able to ride for fear of the unknown. I only need to know that it does work, and works well. I have to put my trust in the fact, not in my own knowledge. I need not know *how* my God keeps me, only that He *does*. You see, if I tried to understand God and to rationalize Him I would never be able to trust Him. Without trust, I could never enjoy the gifts and blessings He has for me. If I never got up on that bike seat as a small boy, I would have never experienced the miracle of cycling. *"Trust in the Lord with all thine heart; and lean not unto thine own understanding. In all thy ways acknowledge Him, and He shall direct thy paths. Be not wise in thine own eyes; fear the Lord, and depart from evil."* Proverbs 3:5-7

No, I don't know how God made the heavens and the earth, but I do know that HE did it. How do I know? The more I ride, the more I know that the wonderful, caring, loving, powerful, and personal God rides with me.

Chapter 2

IN THE BEGINNING

I said in the Introduction that I speak from lessons of error. That is absolutely true. When I began cycling seriously back in the late seventies I made every possible mistake. But, Old Professor Oops is a master teacher. I have learned much through humility and expense: lots of both. Walking to the nearest pay phone at dusk in cycling shoes gives a person lots of time to think about what went wrong. Those lessons sink in deeply.

In the early years I was the poster boy for Phreads United. Phreads (pronounced Freds) are the Master Geeks of the cycling world. Phreads wear the most unstylish attire available, they attach every useless gadget on the market to their bikes, and they have their bikes sized and adjusted to the most uncomfortable riding position imaginable. You may recognize a Phread by

IN THE BEGINNING

his or her tennis shorts, baggy T-shirt, knee length socks, running shoes, and a too-big helmet. They are also adorned with mirrors on the eyeglasses, helmet and/or handlebars. Their riding position normally includes a too-small frame and the saddle height adjusted way, way too low. Look for the knees rising above the chest. Add a cargo rack and maybe a handlebar bag to the mix and you have a master Phread. Yes, I've come a long way.

As a neophyte cyclist I didn't have the slightest clue where to start or what to do. I bought an "adult" bicycle from a discount store, and I was off like a road warrior. Now, this was no simple task. I am by birthright a very, very careful shopper. My family might say I'm the definition of a tightwad. I think that's a little harsh, but let's say I do defiantly research prices. God wants for us to be good stewards of the resources he gives us you know. I'll stick with the terms careful shopper and good steward. That first bike-buying expedition lasted several weeks and took me to every discount store on the Mississippi Gulf Coast at least twice. I ended up getting the "expensive" one for $89.00. I almost settled for the $85 one, but I thought I'd go big-shot for once. It was a beautiful, blue 26-inch "Adult" 10-speed with inch and an eighth "road" tires. Boy, was I proud of "Trigger." I name my bikes, and Trigger was named for the cowboy actor Roy Rogers's loyal companion and famed horse. I was disappointed to learn that most of the younger set didn't know who Trigger was and certainly didn't understand the connection.

I knew nothing of frame height or wheel sizes. Saddle height and riding position escaped my attention along with stem length, bar width, or crank-arm length. I was a proud cyclist. I soon "upgraded" the standard cotton cloth handlebar tape and fitted a rubber-like bar covering that had to be greased and forced onto the bars. Big mistake! Oh yes, I did add the Phread endorsed rear cargo rack with saddlebags and the matching handlebar bag. I had "stuff" to carry you know.

Four years, two salvaged bikes, and lots of painful miles later, I bought a new Centurion from a professional bike shop in San Diego. That bike was my first experience with a frame from a real bike shop and with one that actually fit me. I felt so important when the guy at the bike shop measured me before he showed me anything. I also felt slightly uncomfortable. Part of the sizing is an inseam measurement. I wasn't ready for that one in a bike shop. Okay, I said I was new at this bike thing. Then, to my amazement, he adjusted it specifically to my physique. He set the saddle height and fore/aft position and fitted it with the proper stem length for my reach. It was a fine bike. I paid a whopping $207 including tax and a kickstand for "Trigger II" and I honestly thought that it would last me forever. I told Margaret, my wife, "That's the last bike I'll ever have to buy." Little did I realize that it was only the beginning.

That was when I really began to appreciate cycling and to understand that I had a great deal to learn about bikes and riding. I was an eager pupil.

As time went by and miles piled up, I read and studied everything I could find on cycling. I talked to everyone I met that seemed like they either knew more than me (not a difficult search) or had better equipment than me (not a difficult search). I tried every technique I heard about. Some worked; some were hilarious failures. As I grew in knowledge and experience I also grew stronger. I began to gradually lose the Phread image and gain an ever-increasing appreciation of the sport.

Now, all these years later, I have a driving desire to see novice cyclists begin properly and avoid the long learning curve that I endured. One old adage that I have tortured my children with throughout the years is "There is a proper way to do everything." Cycling is proof positive of this motto. When someone asks my advice I have to restrain myself. Otherwise I overwhelm them with information. Although I thoroughly enjoyed "Trigger" and all the other bikes and adventures in the early years, I would like for others to avoid the frustrating and costly blunders I made.

My advice starts at the very beginning: what bike to buy and where to buy it. Avoid discount store bikes. Discount store bikes tend to be made of lower grade materials and fitted with poor quality components such as brakes and shifting mechanisms. Now, it took me a couple of years to understand that principle. Riding in Spain, I noticed that once in a while a local cyclist would give Trigger an intense and lengthy look-over. I was so proud that even European cyclists appreciated the quality and caliber of such a fine bike. Little did I understand at that time that they were most likely wondering why someone would even attempt to venture out of town on such an unreliable, heavy, ill-sized anchor. Ignorance is bliss.

Those inexpensive material and design factors of low priced bikes make for a heavy, non-responsive bike with drastically decreased dependability. Substandard brakes may add to the excitement as well as one's spontaneous prayer life. When the gears don't shift properly and the breaks don't stop efficiently cycling is an aggravation, not a pleasure. The cheaper bike may save money, but it usually ends up taking up valuable garage

IN THE BEGINNING

space, gathering dust, and not ridden. That isn't much of a bargain now is it?

So, my first advice to a new rider is to buy your bike from an established, reputable bike shop. One size fits all does not apply to bicycles. "Adult" is not a size. Quality bike manufacturers supply a wide selection of frame types, materials, and sizes. Characteristics differ from manufacturer to manufacturer and the bike shop professionals can direct you to the best style, brand, and size that will complement your shape and goals. Minute differences in sizing and adjustments make monstrous differences to comfort and efficiency. Most quality manufacturers offer a wide selection of frame sizes graduated in one or two centimeter increments. Two centimeters in frame size can mean the difference between riding every available chance and having a very expensive metal sculpture hanging in your garage. Experienced shop staff can measure you and take note of your riding goals in order to place you on the proper frame with the best-suited components at an affordable price. After you decide on a bike, they will make all the final adjustments that will not only make riding more comfortable but more efficient. Even if you already own a good bike, go to a reputable shop and ask them to help you with adjustments.

SADDLE SORE SPIRITUALITY

Reputable shops rely on their reputations for continued business. Therefore, you can feel confident that they want to give you a good product and professional service. You will find that most shops carry only quality bikes, components and accessories. Though shops do tend to promote one or two specific brands much like automobile dealerships, you will find that they will make every attempt to place you on the one best suited for you. My experience has been that the sales person is more interested in getting you on the best bike for *you* rather than the most expensive one on the floor. I understand that many people are afraid to go to a specialty bike shop because of lack of knowledge, experience and fear that the sales person will attempt to put you on an overpriced bike. I assure you, of all the shop owners I have known, they all try to put a customer on the proper bike at the least cost. That's a hard concept to adjust to. We are conditioned to mistrust sales people. Bike shops are a refreshing exception. Honestly, the shop owners I have known are among the most honest of business professionals. Of course, I am personally drawn like a magnet to the high-dollar ride. Couple that with my tight fists and deep pockets (you can actually save money if your pockets are deeper than your fingers can reach) and the sales person is about to have a miserable day.

IN THE BEGINNING

Just like the frames they sell, good shops outfit their bikes with reliable components. You will rarely find steel wheels for example or low quality Derailers and other components in a good shop. Special alloy wheels are not only lighter and stronger they are safer. Derailers (the gadgets that shift the gears) must be high quality, light, and accurate or riding will be frustrating enough to keep you off your bike and in front of the TV. I have experienced bikes changing gears on their own. That will raise the excitement level, especially on a hard climb. My first Centurion had a frightening habit of doing that on a particularly steep hill in Balboa Park in San Diego. It was an especially steep hill on the west side of the park that I felt obligated to attempt on a regular basis. Of course when the bike decided to shift itself it did not shift down to an easier gear; it shifted up a couple of cogs to an unmanageable gear. That would bring me to a tenuous stop and a retreat back down to try again. Getting started on a steep hill at that time was impossible for me. Shops will outfit their products with good to excellent components.

I learned the steel wheel lesson early in my cycling education in Mississippi on "Trigger." Remember "Trigger" cost a whopping $89 and the best upgrade was that rubber-like handlebar grip.

Bicycle brakes work by a caliper that clinches the wheel rim. You see, a steel wheel; especially a shiny, chromed one is pretty but loses almost all of its breaking ability once it gets wet: even a little wet. Alloy wheel materials are much, much more reliable in wet conditions. Trigger had shinny steel wheels. I was riding home from the Navy Base and trying desperately to make it home before an afternoon shower soaked me. To this day I hate to ride in the rain. About a hundred yards from the house I felt the first cold, hard raindrops. I could see the real rain bouncing off the street ahead and racing me to the dry safety of my garage. As luck would have it, the garage door was open and no car was in the way. The sprint was on! I jumped out of the saddle like I was on the Champs-Elysee on the last lap of the Tour De France. I lost. The rain hit me just as I jumped the curb and cut across the now wet front lawn. Margaret was out, so no car sat in the garage. Okay, I could still avoid maximum soak if I could just get to the driveway and brake hard as I entered the dry garage. That was a good plan. I cleared the grass, got onto the concrete drive, grabbed both brake levers and slid back on the saddle expecting the force of the breaking to push me forward on the bike. Nothing happened. No hard push forward on the saddle. Uh oh! I'm hitting what seemed like thirty miles per hour with twenty-five feet of pavement left. I squeezed with a death grip on the levers. Nothing. The whole ordeal probably took less than five seconds, but it felt like several minutes to me. It was one of those experiences that unfolds in the mind like a slow reading book. Every detail seemed like it took an eternity, and every scary detail held maximum awareness. As the garage wall rapidly approached, the thought actually and distinctly went through my mind "boy, this is going to hurt!" That thought was followed quickly by a visual of the hole in the wall where my head would be embedded. How was I going to explain this to the landlord? My wife? Trigger kept going like a runaway stallion. About a third of the way into the garage the wheels dried and the brakes began to ever so gradually grip. Nonetheless that wall was coming at me like a slow moving freight train. I imagined my going over the handlebars and my head lodging into the wall. Really! The death grip was still on. My forearms were now hurting from the unrelenting grasp I kept on the brake levers. That old bike gradually slowed like it was trying to teach me a lesson. It stopped with a very distinct and solid "thump" into the wall. Whew! Feet down: take a deep breath. No damage. I'm certain that I saw the two angels waiting for me at the back wall of that garage who stopped me just short of destruction. They were laughing. Alloy wheels are a necessity.

So, (1) Buy the best bike you can afford. (2) Buy it from a reputable bike shop. (3) Let the shop staff put you on the right style and size. (4) Insist on alloy wheels!

Now that you have your shiny new bike it's off on the road to freedom, adventure, and great health. You mount the saddle and stomp the pedal for your first tour expecting hours and hours of smooth riding today. The first thing you learn is that even with the very best of equipment and accessories you were not ready for your first ride since you were a kid. Your legs feel like knotted logs, your lungs feel like burning embers of a campfire, and your bottom is...well you make up the rest of that sentence. It hurts! You try several more excursions over the following days and although you are getting better, you submit to the fact that there must be a better way to do this. And, you now notice that you have the beginnings of a little skin lesion, a sore, where sores are not at all welcome. Now, you understand where the title for this book comes from.

So, where does one acquire the expertise of cycling? Several sources immediately come to mind with this book being the number one option. You can go to Books-A-Million and find

IN THE BEGINNING

any number of good reference texts on cycling. I do recommend reading as much as you can on cycling. Be careful though. Cycling books tend to specialize. You will find books on cycle touring which will guide you in the direction of long distance touring and camping out along the road. You will find books devoted to cycle racing alongside the touring ones. These are great references even for those who never plan to turn a pedal in competition. Most of the techniques needed for racing are beneficial to everyday riding as well. Racing drives us to be ultra efficient with every gram of energy. That concept transfers directly to all levels of riding. However, many cycle racing authors like to go into very regimented and demanding drills, training schedules, and diets. Often they go way beyond the needs of most of us regular people. So, if you do read the books, understand that the advice is very often directed at a specific group of cyclists.

Good cycling magazines are scarce. The better cycling magazines are published in Great Britain and Europe with many of the European periodicals available here in English language versions. However, they tend to be strongly targeted to reporting on international racing events. They do a wonderful job of reporting on the latest racing innovations and events, but may overwhelm a beginning rider. Cycling magazines, like most other periodicals, are informative on a surface level. That is, they don't go in-depth enough into a topic to be of much lasting benefit. I'm not discouraging your reading magazines; I'm just saying you should be open minded and diverse in your approach.

The next best source of cycling knowledge, however, is other riders. Where do you find other riders? The bike shop! Hmmmm, are we seeing a pattern here? Bike shop owners have access to the newest components and accessories and are more than eager to tell you about them. You will find too that most of the employees in the shops are riders too. What a great way to make a living. Bike junkies hang out in bike shops just like motorcyclists hang out... well, where ever they hang out. You will find every degree of cyclist in the shop from a newbie like yourself to the hottest Cat II racer in town. Guess what, they all are chomping at the bit to talk "Rid'n'." Ask away! Don't worry; the shop does not mind you hanging around. The more you learn the more you grow. The more you grow the more you buy. Get the idea?

Bikes shops too are often the clubhouses for cycle clubs. Most shops sponsor a local club and/or a racing team. You will find too that most shops sponsor weekly group training rides in association with the local club. Hmmmm, more "other riders." And, in most cases, those weekly training rides field subgroups that reflect varying abilities. You can expect to see a beginners' group, an intermediate group of more experienced riders, and a blow-your-lungs-out group. The beginners' usually go shorter distances and ride at a slower pace. Most groups, except possibly for the blow-your-lungs-out group, promise not to drop anyone. That is, they will not charge ahead and leave you struggling by yourself to find your own way back home. Groups have ride leaders who are responsible for the safety of the group, keeping the group on course, and assisting anyone with difficulty. You might call these ride leaders the deacons of the Cycling Church Of The Spoken World.

The very best source of riding knowledge is to ride and to ride with someone. All the book knowledge in the world and all the conversations in the shop can't substitute for getting on that bike and putting wind in your face. I have known good athletes who spend the winter months in the gym and in spinning classes. When spring comes, they are not nearly as road-ready as the guys who ride—even if only a few miles a week—year around. I am not saying that cross training is not good. It is. But riding well requires riding often.

Ride with others. You will find that you learn by just observing others: good or bad. You will scrutinize the techniques of those you ride with. You will find that by riding with others you will quickly identify those who are good and improving versus those who are speeding headlong to the world of the phreads. Everyone wants to tell you how well they are doing and how they did it. You will learn just by watching everything they do from their position on the bike to the equipment they use to gear choice.

I used to ride with a very strong young man from Columbia. He could ride like the wind on flat road, but once the asphalt headed uphill he struggled to exhaustion. His problem was that he tried to use all of his muscle power (and he had awesome leg muscle) on the climbs. He had read all the books on proper climbing technique that teach us to ride smaller gears with faster pedal speed while climbing. That just didn't make sense to Rudy. So he tried to power up every little incline. By the end of a twenty-mile ride, he was done in. I remember riding with him one Sunday and trying to coach him on climbing. Finally near the end of the ride, I think only to shut me up; he shifted way down on an especially tough hill. Exhausted as he was at that point he shot up that hill leaving the rest of us in his wake. From that day on, Rudy was a climber! We had created a monster! I don't know if I was proud that the student had beaten the teacher or frightened that I had created a mighty challenger to myself. Had he not ridden with us and been able to learn that little technique he may have eventually given up on cycling. Rudy was one of about five of us who would ride together for several more years. We all improved.

I spent years riding alone and improving but improving very slowly. One season of riding with friends and on group rides improved my ability more than anything I had done previously. I still love to ride by myself, but I also love the experience and challenge of riding with someone who is just a little better than me. If I feel my performance failing, I make a point of hooking up with some tough group rides. As with most other endeavors in life, whether it's sports, career or life in general we improve by partnering ourselves with someone just a little better. Ride occasionally with someone better than yourself, and you will see yourself improving noticeably.

So, (1) Ride. (2) Ride with others. (3) Hang out at the bike shop, and (4) insist on alloy wheels.

Now, how do we and where do we begin our spiritual life and what does cycling have to do with it?

He does not expect us to learn His ways from discount store books, tapes, and simple little lessons. After all, books are written by struggling men who are many times seeking answers to the same problems that the reader is struggling with. Be careful too, just as some cycling authors will give you incorrect or too-specific advice, some religious authors will give you advice that does not fit your needs. Bad cycling advice may get you stranded twenty miles from home. Bad spiritual advice can cost you a closer relationship with God. Like advice we get from various cycling sources we want to check it out before we stake our spiritual life on it. God has provided us with the perfect guidebook. He tells us to study the scriptures: the absolute, authoritative source of spiritual life. Cycling magazines, touring books, and racing books are excellent sources of knowledge for riders, but God has gone one giant leap more by providing *"the" mas*ter reference: the Bible. Oh yes, devotional books and Christian motivational materials are okay, but the *real* source of spiritual stability and growth is His Word. Go there first. Go there often. Go there last. *"Study to show thyself approved unto God, a workman that needeth not to be ashamed, rightly dividing the word of truth. [16]But shun profane and vain babblings: for they will increase unto more* *ungodliness.:"* 2 Timothy 2:15-16. When you read other references and other authors, check out what you are being taught against the standard: the Bible. When you are riding with others you are doing the same thing. You observe the good techniques and use them; you take note of the bad techniques and avoid them. *"And Jesus answering said unto them, do ye not therefore err, because ye know not the scriptures, neither the power of God?"* Mark 12:25

Jesus started his ministry by going to the Temple. What was the Temple? The Temple was the place where the rabbis met. It was the place where the people gathered to worship and to learn the scriptures and to seek atonement by blood sacrifice. If a person desired to know God, the place to go was the Temple. People—even Jesus—sat and listened to the "experts" of the day. If you want to know cycling you go to the place where cyclists gather: the bike shop. If you want to know spiritual truths and meet spiritual friends, and observe spiritual things go to the place where Christians gather: the church. *"Forsake not the gathering of yourselves together."* You will find every degree of Christian in the church from a newbie like yourself to the hottest preacher, teacher, prophet, healer, etc. in town. Guess what, they all are chomping at the bit to talk "Jesus" to you. Ask away! Don't worry; the pastor does not mind you hanging around. The more you learn the more you grow. The more you grow the more the Kingdom grows. Get the idea?

And, the very best way to grow spiritually is to fellowship with other Christians. Again, Hebrews 10:25 says *"Not forsaking the assembling of ourselves together, as the manner of some is; but exhorting one another: and so much the more, as ye see the day approaching."* After Jesus' assention into heaven, the Apostils stayed together helping each other. They went out into all the world alone? Nope, they went in pairs. I wonder why? Maybe it was to learn from one another and to encourage one another. Throughout the Bible we find example after example of saints growing through fellowship with saints. We also find examples of Bible figurers struggling alone. *"The way of a fool is right in his own eyes: but he that hearkeneth unto counsel is wise"* Proverbs 12:15.

God desires for us to begin our spiritual journey by equipping ourselves the best way we possibly can. He said, *"But seek ye first the kingdom of God, and his righteousness; and all these things shall be added unto you* Matthew 6:33. So what is "the Kingdom of God?" Among other things, the Kingdom represents and is the best of everything. It has mansions. It has streets of gold. It has no pain or suffering. It is the seat where all knowledge and wisdom resides. It is the source of all that is good. It has alloy wheels. It's where the Saints of Glory hang out. Seek ye a good bike shop: Seek ye first the Kingdom of God.

So, (1) use and study the Bible as your spiritual guide. (2) Gather where other people gather for spiritual fellowship: the church. (3) Talk, walk, fellowship with other Christians. (4) Insist on alloy wheels.

Chapter 3

KEEP THE LOAD EASY

I have just finished watching for the umpteenth time my DVD of the 2003 Tour De France that I think was the best Tour ever staged—at least the best one I have ever witnessed. I watch that film while I ride the resistance trainer indoors. It inspires me. The '03 Tour was the closest of the seven contests between two of the greatest riders to ever battle on the roads of France: Lance Armstrong and Jan Ullrich. They tested each other every day for three weeks and across two mountain ranges. Lance crashed; Jan crashed. Lance suffered a day in the mountains; Jan suffered a day in the mountains. Lance won a time trial; Jan won a time trial. Mere seconds separated the two throughout the 2,300-mile challenge. The victory was not sealed until the last miles of the last day of competition. Not only did it match the strategy, fitness, and determination of these two great riders, but it also matched two basic and opposing theories of riding technique.

Ullrich, the great German rider, has enormously powerful legs and uses them to his advantage. His riding style is one in which he uses a slower, more powerful cadence (pedal speed) with big gears to force himself to the very top of the sport. Armstrong, on the other hand, rides with his trademark high-speed cadence. The difference may go unnoticed by the casual observer, but to the knowledgeable student of cycling it is as different as a Mercedes diesel and a Ford GT40. They both go very fast but with very different styles.

The initial instinct of all new riders is to prove to self and society how in shape and strong they are. After all, great athletes are powerful individuals who use their brute strength to conquer all obstacles and to impress the girls. And, the girls like to prove that they are just as capable as any man on the road. Couple that with how almost all of us learned to ride as children: on heavy single speed Schwinns. The standard old kids' bike offered only one option for motivation: lots of muscle power and no gear choices. That's fine when you are seven and have more energy than any ten adults. That technique will put the average adult Sunday afternoon athlete in a Bark-a-lounger for a month.

My very first advice to a newbie rider once on the road is to forget the macho image and concentrate on efficiency. I understand that most of us learned to ride a bike as a child, but most of us didn't learn to ride *properly* as a child. Remember, "There is a proper way to do everything?" There is a proper way to pedal a bike, and it is probably not the way you learned as a kid or the way you imagine you should ride now.

Since you are the engine, you must learn to use your engine to its best advantage. Now if you're a Jan Ullrich type with legs like hydraulic pistons and lungs with the capacity of oil drums you can pursue his style. Most of us don't possess anything close to that kind of physiology. I've tried that approach and for me it was neither efficient nor healthy nor pleasant.

Note that modern adult bikes have a selection of gears. The old ten-speed has evolved into the eighteen, twenty, and in some cases even the thirty speeds. You have a multitude of choices, but most beginners tend to pick a gear, a macho gear, and stick with it.

An engine, any engine (remember, you are the engine of your bike), operates best and most efficiently within a narrow speed range. That is the engine speed, not the vehicle speed. It produces most of its power and torque within a few

KEEP THE LOAD EASY

revolutions per minute (RPMs). Run an engine too slow and it stalls out and wastes fuel, power, and causes mechanical damage. Run it too fast and wastes fuel, power, and causes more mechanical damage.

I remember way back in the sixties a guy in Florida took a standard full size Ford and modified it to run on hydraulic motors through a series of hydraulic energy storing devices. A standard Ford six cylinder engine powered the whole thing. He calculated the most efficient speed for that engine and governed it for that specific speed. Hydraulic motors controlled the road speed. In its standard form that car would be lucky to achieve twenty miles per gallon of fuel. But, by restricting the engine to its most efficient speed it traveled Florida roads quite handily at nearly 100 MPG!

Since you are the bike's engine the same principle applies to you and your legs. For some strange reason the brain seems to think the body is not carrying it's fair share if muscles are not heavily stressed. Not true for the cyclist. If you pound those leg muscles too heavily for too many miles you will end up calling your best friend to rescue you where you collapsed at the side of some strange country road in the middle of nowhere. This may be the hardest lesson for the new cyclist to learn. KEEP THE CADENCE—LEG

SPEED—UP! FASTER LEG SPEED IS BETTER. Learn to pedal at a faster pace than your brain thinks you should. Let's don't make this ridin' thing harder than it should be. Don't worry about your road speed, at least in the beginning. Road speed will improve as your fitness and experience grows. Imagine that you are a very small ultra-economy car with a grossly undersized engine. For me, that doesn't take much imagination. To keep that car running, you must keep the engine revved up. That's why they put four, five, and six speed transmissions in cars. You can choose the gear that best suits the situation while keeping the engine revs up.

The same principle applies to cycling. Keep the leg speed up. Use all of those twenty or so gears to achieve that. When the road goes upward, shift down to an easier gear and keep your leg speed up. Once over the top, click up a gear or two and keep pedaling. If you try and muscle your way up every hill, you won't last the ride. Remember Rudy? He was strong as a young bull but he tortured himself on the climbs until he discovered this simple and basic skill.

Some racing cyclists ride a fixed gear single speed rear wheel during the off-season. They pick an easy gear that forces them to keep the cadence high. The fixed gear, however, means that it won't freewheel. Freewheeling is coasting but the pedals don't go around. It's designed into the rear hub so that you can coast without moving the pedals. Hear that musical clicking from the rear wheel? That's the freewheel hub singing to you. So, not only does the fixed gear force a high cadence while pedaling, it forces the high leg speed all the time—even slowing down. Some coaches seem to think more leg speed and less muscle power during the colder winter months helps prevent leg muscle injuries. It certainly conditions racers' leg speed and enforces a smooth and steady pedal stroke. Riding a fixed wheel does take some practice however. You see, after riding a freewheel all season you automatically expect the thing to coast when you stop pedaling. NOT! Those pedals just keep on a turnin'. It's like riding a revolving door. Once you're there the thing won't stop and there's no way out. Good cycling gloves are an excellent idea, because you have a splendid opportunity of an up close and personal interview with the pavement in front. That fixed wheel will throw you like a Texas bull! Create in your mind's eye a vision of the term "face plant."

Even more common is the proliferation of spinning classes at the local gym. The don't-I-look-trendy set spends hundreds of dollars a year to sit on a stationary bike in a hot, stinky (but trendy) gym and pedal at a high cadence while some super-athletic chick plays loud, fast music and insults your inability to keep up. Spinning classes achieve great results, but I prefer to torture myself in private.

Okay, so you ask what is the proper cadence? It depends. How's that for a non-answer? Let me explain with the car engine analogy again. A 1.6 liter Mazda four cylinder engine has different characteristics from, let's say, a 3.8 liter Ford V-six. And, those two engines behave differently depending on the car style to which they are mated, the load they are expected to carry, and the terrain in which they are driven. You and your bike have similar variables. Are you riding a road bike or a mountain bike? Is your bike a sixteen-pound lightweight or a thirty-pound cruiser? Are you riding up Mount Evans or down the Florida coast? These variables will direct your cadence range.

There are some less confusing guidelines though. Please keep in mind that these are guidelines—starting points—and you will need to establish your own most efficient style. Both Lance Armstrong and Jan Ullrich are awesome cyclists but have developed different styles based on their individual physical characteristics. However, understand that the overwhelming error most new cyclists make is pushing too big of a

KEEP THE LOAD EASY

gear with too much muscle. Faster and easier is better. But in most cases try to keep the leg speed between about 60 and 100 RPM. Ride above 60 RPM on reasonably flat roads or easy rolling hills and under about 100 on the down hills and on fast roads. Anything less than 60 is generally demanding too much muscle. Spin much more than 100 in the beginning and you are losing power. That 100 cadence will increase the more proficient and experienced you become. Of course the 60 rule goes out the window half way up that twelve percent grade just outside of town. And, the 100 rule will dwindle on the return trip. I'll talk more about hills and climbing in later chapters.

Now I imagine your next question is how do I know what my cadence is? I have two primitive and one hi-tech answer. The first primitive method is that your legs will tell you. Oh yes, your legs can talk and talk loudly. When you consciously notice each and every pedal stroke you are pedaling way too slow. Your thighs will start to burn and your knees will whisper, "You are killing me." Can you hear them? The pain isn't usually severe; it is more nagging. If you are pedaling as fast as you think you can but the bike is under running your effort, you have chosen much too small gearing and your cadence is too high. Be careful not to spin your kneecaps off. You may notice that your knees now want to separate your lower from your upper leg bones. Ouch! Shift up. At the top end, you want to feel a perceptible resistance on the pedals.

For method two let's go back to Chapter two and re-read the part about riding with others. When you ride with experienced friends, take note of their leg speed and compare that to yours while you are on the road. This is really a good indicator since it takes into account two important variables. One is experience: your friend's not yours. The more you or your friend has ridden the more proper cadence becomes second nature. The other factor is the situation at hand. Observe how your friend changes cadence as conditions change. How do they ride an easy hill: a steep hill? How about headwinds verses assist winds? Observe. Emulate.

Now for the hi-tech method: go back to the bike shop and ask about computers. No, don't panic. I don't want you to carry a Dell laptop on your handlebars. Cycling computers are great little devices about the size of a pocket watch that attach to the handle bar. Depending on how hi-tech you want to go and how much you are willing to spend, computers will give you a wealth of information. A basic cycling computer will give you road speed, distance traveled, elapsed trip time, average speed, and a few more bragable little bits of data. On the upper end of the price scale they will add such features as gear-inch calculations, wireless transmitters, heart rate monitors, calories burned; and yes, our old friend cadence. You can know exactly what your cadence is at any point. You may be amazed to know how slow your pedal speed actually is. The cadence feature, I feel, is well worth the modest investment to the novice rider. It will tell you at a glance when you need to shift up or down. I like to use a computer with a cadence feature in the off-season when I'm forced indoors and onto the resistance trainer. It keeps me honest. I seldom use one out on the road. I have ridden enough over the years to sense proper leg speed by instinct. For the newbie, a good computer with a cadence feature is a wise investment. It could help prevent many days off the bike nursing sore legs.

I'll bet by now you're wondering what leg speed and cadence has to do with your spiritual journey. How many Christians do you know who are exhausting themselves in their Christian life. You will see them in Sunday school, morning worship, evening worship, mid-week prayer meeting, and every other time the doors are opened. They join the choir; they volunteer for nursery and every other job opening available. The list goes on and on. Do you see yourself here at all? Are any of these things wrong? No, absolutely not! Do they all add to the Kingdom of God and enhance your spiritual life? Yes, without a doubt! Will this Christian-life pace cause spiritual burnout over a prolonged period of time? Very likely yes, I think.

We have all been given spiritual talents and gifts to carry us through our spiritual lives and to use to further the Kingdom of God. Many of us want to travel with *ALL* the talents and gifts all at once: in other words overload our spiritual legs. Then what happens? We end up on the side of some strange spiritual country road in the middle of spiritual nowhere having to call our best friend to come and rescue us.

God, through the Holy Spirit, has given us tasks that match perfectly with our skills, talents, gifts, and abilities. He knows just how much of a load our holy legs can stand and still continue on the journey. Run your spiritual life too slow and it stalls out, wastes fuel, wastes power, and causes soul damage. Run your spiritual life too fast and it stalls out, wastes fuel, wastes power, and causes soul damage. We don't need to try and be a Mercedes diesel when God has made us to be a GT40. He can quite adequately handle all the other tasks he has not specifically assigned to us and provided the ability to complete. He says so in 2 Corinthians 11:9, *"My grace is sufficient for thee: for My strength is made perfect in weakness."* HIS strength is made perfect in whose weakness: yours and mine. He has given us the strengths and abilities that HE has known we will need even before the foundation of the earth. HE fills in those voids that he already knows we have. Perfect! Oh, God has made some of us to be Mercedes Diesels; and if you are one of those, power on! Jan Ullrich has a much different style than Armstrong, but he knew his abilities and maintained his position at the top of pro cycling for many years. How do you maintain your spiritual position? David tells us in Psalms 55, *"Cast thy burden upon the Lord, and He shall sustain thee: He shall never suffer the righteous to be moved."*

So how do we know what spiritual cadence is correct? The Holy Spirit will tell you. He does speak you know. Get into the Word and study it with the Holy Spirit. He is your little computer and will give you all sorts of valuable information.

Oh yes, Jan Ullrich has been a top cycling professional for over a decade. He was the German Cycling Champion and has won most of the prestigious races in the world. He has an Olympic Gold medal and he won the World Amateur Cycling Championship. He won the Tour De France once and has been second five times. Some have called him the strongest cyclist in the world. Lance Armstrong, a Professional World Cycling Champion, won seven consecutive Tours De France. No one else in the history of the race has won more than five. He has won the World Championship and has completely dominated the European Spring Classics. He retired at the apex of his career with the very real possibility that he could have won his eighth Tour De France had he continued. His trademark high-speed cadence has become the standard style that others seem to imitate.

What do you want to be: a GT40 or a Mercedes Diesel? Let me offer you one more little insight. Early in Armstrong's career he was known for his pure strength and lack of finesse. In other words he was as strong as two bulls and about as graceful. Most experts predicted that he could be a great one-day racer in the European classics, but he would not likely be a great tour champion. Many predicted an impressive but short career. A former world-class cyclist turned coach, Chris Carmichael, connected with Armstrong and taught him the now famous trademark spin. You see, he *learned* to pedal efficiently: it wasn't a natural instinct. He learned from a successful veteran who had been where Lance wanted to go. Proper pedaling is a learned skill. Proper spiritual pedaling may be a learned skill as well. Where do we learn spiritual skills? How about those mature, stable Christians in your life? Peter tells us in 1 Peter 5:5, *"Likewise, ye younger, submit yourselves unto the elder. Yea, all of you be subject one to another, and be clothed with humility: for God resisteth the proud, and giveth grace to the humble."* Learn from one another. Learn from the elders who have sustained experience and display fruitful spiritual lives. You may be spiritually as devoted and willing as Paul, but will your spiritual career be impressive but short? Are you a Mercedes diesel or a GT40?

Chapter 4

A PROPER WAY TO DO EVERYTHING

Once you get into this cycling thing you will start to notice that your "uncycled" friends and acquaintances will begin an endless string of mindless comments and questions. "Do you wear those tight, skinny bike shorts?" "How can you sit on that little seat?" "What do you mean you actually ride out on the BIG road? The one I like is, "I'd ride if I had a big soft seat to sit on." The truth is, that person probably already has a big soft seat and constantly sits on it.

Now, we must admit that to the casual observer our attire and equipment may seem to have been devised by a sadistic throwback to the Spanish Inquisition. And, the very idea of riding 25, 50, maybe 100 miles on roads designed for car traffic may seem a little ambitious to the cycle-resistant intellectual. When they find out that we aggressively seek out the toughest mountain passes to ride for fun and challenge that really seals their diagnosis of our need for professional help. "Do you *reeeeealllly* ride up Skyreach Mountain?" That phrase (or some derivative thereof) is generally followed by silence, a slight shake of the head, and a blank gaze way past you. They don't use these exact words, but what they are saying is, "I really don't have the mental ability to comprehend that, but I can't come up with anything more intelligent to say." The comments are very often our cycle-less friends' off-handed way of suggesting that we are not too bright but phrased in the form of a question.

For years I tried to explain why we ride the way we do, leaned over on down-turned handlebars, on skinny treadles tires and wafer thin saddles (it is a saddle, not a seat). I've learned, however, that valid explanations most often fall on unhearing ears. People give the polite facial expression that indicates they are intently engrossed in their enlightenment when all the time they are saying to themselves, "This guy's a total nut case." It seems like a pointless waste of enlightenment. Well, maybe that's like trying to explain the joy of being a Christian to an unsaved soul. No one can understand complete joy in Christ until they accept and experience a personal relationship with Jesus. No one can understand the idiosyncrasies of cycling until they have experienced a long ride on a beautiful spring day or topping a mountain just a moment before complete exhaustion. Actually I've questioned my own sanity when near the end of a 100 mile, six hour ride with legs feeling like tenderized beef and every other part of my body near complete fatigue, and I ponder to myself, "Isn't this fun? I wish this ride were longer." No one can understand that until they have experienced it. Who can understand the joy of Jesus until He has become their personal savior?

At first glance many of the standards associated with cycling do in fact seem—at best—questionable. Spandex shorts? Fingerless gloves? Skinny saddles? Skinnier tires? Down-turned handlebars? We do have some unusual paraphernalia. Many of our accessories just do not make sense even to some who have been involved in the sport for years. Let's admit it. Twenty millimeter tires with 120 PSI of air pressure does not exactly evoke visions of comfort. However, I can assure you that cycling's idiosyncrasies all have a distinct and intelligent purpose.

If cycling's traditions were to be traced over its long history they would reveal a refining progression of very clever design and technique. For the most part, cycling has simply used technology to perfect its basic foundation.

Refinements do not always take a direct path. Innovations are not always positive. Over the past thirty or so years, I have seen lots of creative gadgets come along. Many have gone by the wayside along with lots of my money spent trying them out. For instance, I have seen a variety of saddle designs come and go from the oversized tractor seat design to the double pedestal model with movable pads: one for each cheek. The time tested slim racing saddle survives. And, I went through a few years of trendy handlebar tape that more resembled Christmas packaging ribbon than bar tape. It was pretty and colorful, but incredibly dangerous. Holding cellophane-like wrappings on your bars, once wet from sweat, is about as easy as driving a truck with an icicle. Bar tape is meant to provide a sure grip and some comfort from pavement-induced vibrations. The cute little tape trend didn't last long, and the most popular wrap has reverted back to a refined but original cork. Cork is superb for absorbing moisture, providing a sound gripping surface, and dampening road shock. Its design and characteristics serve a distinct purpose.

Oh yes, there was the top-of-the-bar brake lever extension. Some manufacturers even named it a "Safety Lever." Supposedly this attachment made braking safer by allowing the rider to brake with the hands on top of the handlebar. It worked marginally well under easy, casual breaking. However, under hard breaking—say an emergency situation like rocketing toward the back wall of the garage—the extension levers flexed like rubber shovel handles and in some cases broke off! Safer? No! Do I speak from experience? Yes! I could go on and on, but you get the idea.

Now, I am certainly not saying that we have not seen wonderful innovations. We have. For instance the evolution of the shifter lever progressed from the down tube mounted, full friction lever to the down tube mounted "indexed" lever: "click shifting." The original lever required that the rider lean over and move the lever fore or aft until the correct gear was achieved and then tweak it to its final position. It required concentration and a fine touch. Try doing that at twenty miles per hour in a group of ten or twelve riders while exiting a hard right hand turn. Now we have ergo shifters mounted on the brake levers where our hands rest anyway, and they are indexed "Click & Shift" so we get crisp, precise gear changes. Wonderful! The purpose and the concept remain the same: a shifter that is precise, handy, positioned to be accessible, lightweight, and capable of addressing multiple gears. Refinement of a basic.

We have progressed from leather straps to keep our feet on the pedals to ski binding-like "Clipless" pedals. The purpose is to keep the feet attached to the pedal. They both do a great job of that, but the "clipless" ones make exiting them much less adventuresome. No, I do not know why they are called "clipless" when they in fact clip the shoes/feet to the pedal. I'd think a better name would be "strapless", but I'm not the guy who makes up names for gadgets.

I am old enough to remember wool cycling shorts and jerseys, wood platform shoes, leather helmets, and real chamois leather inserts inside shorts. Wool has given way to Lycra. Wood is replaced by space-age plastics. Synthetic, soft materials have (thank goodness) pushed real leather chamois to a faint, bad memory. New fabrics have replaced wool for shorts and shirts, but the design requirements still remain satisfied: a tight fitting garment that will evaporate moisture. Wood once provided the inflexibility in shoe platforms to limit energy loss from foot flex. Modern plastics and carbon fiber accomplish that today: lighter and cooler. Chamois was once a wonderful material for reducing chaffing, absorbing moisture, and cushioning the saddle. Synthetic chamois are softer, provide better moisture control, support cushioning, and won't become hard and brittle after laundering. Oh yes, real chamois stayed hard and brittle for the first few miles of a ride. We had to condition it with a cream—chamois conditioner—before each ride or it was like straddling a rough-hewn log.

The one thing I have observed is that cycling basics remain cycling basics. Improvements are made, technology comes forward; but the underlying concepts remain valid. Sure, things like saddle material and padding have evolved, but the elements that define a quality saddle remain intact.

I guess the biggest technological advancement has been in helmet design. The leather hairnet has given way to the ultra-light hard shell helmet. It still has to be lightweight and keep the old noggin in one piece and capable of riding another day. But the degree to which it does those things has extremely improved over the past few years.

I am now using computer-based Bible software with something like ten different Bible translations, three different daily devotionals, a dozen or so commentaries, and lots of other features many of which I absolutely do not understand. But, know what? His word remains HIS word! It serves the same needs as it has always served. It is the same God Inspired Scripture that I read in the

A PROPER WAY TO DO EVERYTHING

King James Version fifty years ago. It—no matter what version or how it is presented—has the same message and speaks to the same issues that it did throughout history. The book may be electronic now; the issues may involve modern society, but the message is the same. Basics are basics.

So, let me get back to my point. Why are cycling paraphernalia designed like they are? I think I hear my children way off in the distance chanting, "*There is a proper way to do everything. There is a proper way to do everything, there is a proper way to....*" Since the name of the game in cycling is efficiency, everything has a very specific purpose: nothing more, nothing less.

I am constantly amused by the skeptics who wouldn't be caught dead on a bike but have all the clever advice on what equipment and technique we should use. I can almost hear them now with the slow, country voice offering: "Well ya know I'd get me one of those big ol' fat bicyclin' seats. Ya know the ones with the springs? En, I'd put one of them soft sheepskin covers on it. What da yawl think of that?" They remind me of the non-Christians who constantly instruct and define how a Christian should behave. I wonder how they have become so well versed in spiritual behavior while rarely attending church, reading the Bible, or spending time in prayer.

So why *do* we wear skin-tight shorts and other funny looking clothes? When I started riding, I wore the Phread endorsed running shorts and baggy T-shirts. I suffered for some years with that fashion statement. I finally bought real riding shorts and a fine, yellow cycling jersey while on a port visit in San Remo, Italy. What a difference! What a wonderful difference! You see, regular shorts or jeans (or what have you) don't stay put while pedaling. They tend to ride up and bunch up. The riding up causes friction between the inner thigh and the saddle (it's a saddle remember, not a seat). Friction causes chaffing and chaffing causes pain. And, if that were not enough, loose-fitting garments tend to bunch up near the junction of the saddle, and the rider. Get the picture? After a few short miles, you feel like you are riding on a rope. And, that bunching that causes friction, chaffing, and so on leads to little lesions on parts you really don't want little lesions. Re-read the title of this book. 'Nuff said? We do have a good, non-fashion reason for Lycra shorts. They must be tight, form-fitting, and thin so they stay put. Shirts and all the other garments need to be snug as well. Wind resistance is a big power grabber on the bike. Loose fitting jerseys act like drag chutes and rob you of valuable energy. Now, be careful. The jersey needs to be able to breathe some too. You need to be able to get enough cooling air circulating so you don't overheat, but not so much that you look like the Popin' Dough Boy in Technicolor. The fabric needs to be able to breathe and to wick moisture away from your skin. Wool ironically does a wonderful job of keeping the rider cool, warm and dry. New, modern, hi-tech fabrics have made wool cycling apparel obsolete, and the new materials do a wonderful job. They make you look way stylish too!

So why is the saddle (it's a saddle remember, not a seat) so skinny and hard? I suppose that is the most voiced hostility generated from non-cyclists. In fact, it is occasionally a hostility voiced from me near the end of a long ride. To understand this you must recall that the name of the game in cycling is efficiency, everything has a very specific purpose: nothing more, nothing less. Certainly the "nothing less" part is referring to the saddle issue.

The purpose of the saddle on a bike is not meant for rest and relaxation. It is an important part of proper and efficient cycling. It is part of the whole technique. You see, the best riding position is not sitting upright as you would on a motorcycle. You ride *on* a motorcycle; you *ride* a bicycle. The same correlation applies to riding *on* a horse. The horse or the Harley is doing the

SADDLE SORE SPIRITUALITY

work. With the bike, you are doing the work. So proper position for power transfer is paramount. The most efficient riding position incorporates sharing your weight between the pedals, the handlebar, and the saddle. These are the only points where the body contacts the bike. It is a saddle remember, not a seat. You will want to support about a third of your weight on the pedals. That's how you transfer power to forward travel. Adding your own body weight to the power stroke is a little clever trick in efficiency. Now lean forward and rest your hands on the handlebars. See, placing your upper body weight partly on the bars relieves the load on the...saddle. You will find that having your hands on the bar, either on the tops or on the drops, allows you the leverage to pull somewhat with the arms through the top of the pedal stroke adding—guess what—POWER! So, now you see that your weight is not actually placed fully on the saddle but distributed over the whole bike. The saddle becomes part of the solution, not the problem. If you were to sit totally upright on the saddle for long periods of time, all of your weight will be concentrated on the rather small area known as your "sit bones." As much padding as is provided elsewhere on your posterior, your sit bones area has relatively little cushion. Your one hundred and what-ever pounds on your two little sit bones can cause some discomfort over a few short miles.

I have already talked about the chaffing problem in relation to apparel. Chaffing is a problem too with a wide saddle. You see your inner thighs move in close proximity to the saddle thousands of times during a ride. Each time the legs move, they will rub anything nearby I.E. the saddle. So, if the saddle is too wide, the inner thighs rub against the saddle and we get friction between the inner legs and the saddle. If we get friction we get chaffing and eventually sores. The same holds true for extra soft, spongy saddles; except the friction, chaffing, and so on occur somewhere else...well think about it. Some cushioning is welcome, but too much has the opposite benefit. English made Brooks™ saddles have no padding at all. They are nothing more than thick, high-quality leather stretched over a precision-built frame. Brooks remains one of the most prized saddles on the market. The leather will, over many miles, conform to the contours of the owner's anatomy. It becomes a perfect fit without any padding at all and one of the most comfortable saddles available. Brooks owners will quite often keep the saddle and transfer it from old bike to new bike over the years. The quality is in the fit, not the cushion.

SADDLE SORE SPIRITUALITY

One last thing. You are doing a highly refined balancing act while riding. That saddle is an important part of precision bike handling. You guide a bike not by steering with the handlebars but by minute and gentle leanings of your body. Since the saddle is the highest point of the machine, it gives the most accurate feedback to you the rider about the condition and position of the bike. And, it provides the best point to induce those minute adjustments. A slight body shift at the saddle has the best influence on handling, balance, and direction. It is most effective when descending hills: mountains. The bigger and more cumbersome the saddle, the less effective the bike control. Think about that the next time you are at 45 MPH downhill and you can't exactly see around the curve ahead. Do you want to do your delicate steering with a log or a fine, light tiller?

So, does the skinny saddle make a little more sense now? Okay, I do know that those first few miles on a good bike will produce some (this is a medical term) "discomfort." If you have not ridden in several years, you have conditioned your anatomy to suffer flat and cushy seats. (Seats, not saddles). You body will take a few miles to condition to the contours of the saddle, and the saddle will take a few miles to contour to you. It usually takes about two weeks of regular riding.

After that either the pain goes away or you start to enjoy it. If you start to enjoy the pain you may qualify as a *real cyclist.*

Why skinny, treadles tires? More rubber on the road means more resistance. More resistance means more energy to get down the road. A high-pressure tire—110 PSI and more—helps too.

I'm still learning "proper ways" in cycling. That's the great thing about going to church—uh—group rides. Watch the fruitful Christians—er—strong riders. See how they do things and ask why.

Simple things have a proper way. My son, Michael, taught me how to drink from a water bottle. Now you'd think drinking is drinking, but there is a proper way. I must admit I thought he was being a little compulsive with the drinking lesson. But, I found that it makes a big difference. You see, you want to grab your water bottle from the cage with your fingers pointing downward. Lift the bottle up to your mouth so that you are cradling it with your fingers pointing up. Do not drink with your hand on top of the bottle. Go ahead; try it both ways while riding with a group. If you drink with your hand on top (fingers pointing down or even to the side) you will have to tilt your head way back to drink. How well can you see in front of you? If you drink with your fingers pointing up while cradling the bottle from the bottom, you can tilt the bottle, not your head. You will be able to drink *and* see where you are going. Your riding partners will appreciate this little technique.

The book of Judges gives us the account of Gideon leading the Israelites in war against the Midianites. God told Gideon to take his soldiers to the river to drink.

> *"And the* L ORD *said to Gideon, 'Everyone who laps from the water with his tongue, as a dog laps, you shall set apart by himself; likewise everyone who gets down on his knees to drink.' And the number of those who lapped, putting their hand to their mouth, was three hundred men; but all the rest of the people got down on their knees to drink water. ⁷Then the* L ORD *said to Gideon, 'By the three hundred men who lapped I will save you, and deliver the Midianites into your hand. Let all the other people go, every man to his place.'" Judges 7:4 –7*

God wanted soldiers who could drink and watch for the enemy and danger at the same time. God knows there is a proper way to drink whether on the battlefield or on the bike. Oh yes, those three hundred were victorious.

A PROPER WAY TO DO EVERYTHING

We read too in Matthew the account of Jesus freeing and rebuking a devil from a boy. The Disciples could not deliver the boy, but Jesus did. When questioned why, Jesus answered: *"Howbeit this kind goeth not out but by prayer and fasting."* Matthew 17:2 So; it seems there is a specific, proper way to exorcise that specific type of devil: "...but by prayer and fasting." The Disciples were good, spiritual men, but they were not practicing a proper way to do everything.

The Bible is full, cover to cover, of ways for us to live and live more abundantly. The Ten Commandments are a brief list of flesh and blood proper ways to live. Those principles have never changed. Now the major ones—the biggies—like killing, stealing, and no other gods before me, are about as obvious as the certainty that wheels should be round. But what about the more day-to-day restrictive ones: how do we accept them? You know, like do not covet your neighbor's wife, house, servant, Mercedes and so on. How can coveting ("After all I'm only *'wishing'* I had his Mercedes") be a bad thing? That rule was written way back in Old Testament days and hardly applies in modern, sophisticated society doesn't it? What about that "Do not commit adultery" one? How can that be so bad with today's birth controlled society? And anyway isn't it a victimless crime? Who does it hurt between two consenting adults? How can anything that is so enjoyable (I'm told) be a bad thing? It must be a great thing based on the overwhelming number of participants. Well, God knows that anything less than a focused, committed bond between you and your spouse causes friction. Friction causes chaffing between you and the one God has placed you with. Chaffing causes little relationship lesions which fester, bleed and can become a disabling "saddle sore" to your life. Left unchecked, the end result of adultery can destroy a wonderful life and family. On the surface, it looks like a good thing for physical fulfillment. Truth is that it will cause unimaginable pain to YOU. The righteous God has not given us restrictive commandments; He has given us constructive commandments that will enhance our lives.

God gave the Israelites very specific instructions on how to offer the blood sacrifice for atonement. The Israelites understood, appreciated, and practiced those instructions. They had a good handle on the consequences of not observing the proper way to sacrifice. Left to their own logic they probably would have devised their own method for atonement. It may well have seemed reasonable but the result of their "logic" would have been tragic. Death! Ask Cain if you ever get the chance.

As an example, God has even given specific instructions (a proper way) for how to give: ten percent to be paid by the Children of God into the storehouse. Human reasoning jumps right past that concept, and explains that churchy people ought to "contribute" what they think they can "afford" for the "upkeep" of the church. The care of the poor, the widows, and the orphans and so on after all is the responsibility of the government to be financed through taxes (significantly more than God's proper ten percent). God has offered us the law of tithing for some very valid reasons and many good people are missing the benefits and blessings by not practicing the proper way to handle the gifts God has made available. It is the proper way. Are some wasting huge amounts of financial energy? I can tell you from personal experience that tithing has supernatural benefits.

The unsaved world seems to be able to lecture unceasingly on how to get to heaven. How often have you heard the "I'm a good person" method of salvation? Well, that technique actually sounds like a pretty good idea; kinda like a fat, cushy saddle sounds like a good idea. But, that is not God's perfect design. Romans 6:23 tells us, *"For the wages of sin is death; but the gift of God is eternal life through Jesus Christ our Lord."* Jesus himself said *"He that believeth and is baptized* *shall be saved; but **he that believeth not shall be damned**.*" Mark 16:16. And in John 3:16-17 He tells us, *"For God so loved the world, that he gave his only begotten Son, that **whosoever believeth in him should not perish, but have everlasting life**. ¹⁷For God sent not his Son into the world not to condemn the world; but that the world through him might be saved."* Well, that kind of debunks the old "I'm a pretty good guy" method don't you think? Not only has He set the best way; he has proclaimed the *only* way. Yet we have generations of good, ethical people seeking heaven but going in the opposite direction.

He has given us the Handbook of Proper Ways: The Bible. He has not only given us the guidebook, but he has given us a personal counselor to check with: The Holy Spirit. Let's quit wasting our spiritual energy and seek the proper way to live. You know of course that you will look odd due to that continuous smile on your face, and others will not understand why you do the things you do. Once you get into this Christian thing you will start to notice that your un-Christianed friends and acquaintances will begin an endless string of mindless comments and questions. You will have so much fun, though, telling them why you behave the way you do.

Chapter 5

KEEP YOUR EYES UPON JESUS

Bike handling—getting the bike to go where you want it to go—is a very delicate and subtle activity. Watch a child who is just learning to ride. It is an awkward and often disastrous feat. The natural inclination is to change direction or to even keep going in a straight line by making distinct movements to the handlebar. Except for very slight alterations at very slow speeds, that can result in an abrupt and close-up inspection of the pavement.

You see, bikes are somewhat like boats. They both tend to exhibit unusual handling characteristics. One thing that young Navy officers learn early in their careers is that when they are on the bridge and order the helmsman to turn, that ship is going to roll in the opposite direction of the turn.

In other words, if the ship (it's a ship, not a boat) makes a starboard turn it will roll to port. That's a weird sensation when you go right and left at the same time. If you roll too much with a ship, it capsizes. The same principle applies to a bike, but pavement is less forgiving and much more painful than water. Bikes and boats do not ride on a stable platform. Cars, buses, and other four-wheeled beasts are supported at all four corners and can be steered by turning the wheels. Turn the steering wheel to the right and go right. Turn your handlebars abruptly to the right and your bike, with body attached, will object by throwing you left: and in many cases, down.

Okay then, how then do we steer a bike? For the most part, bikes steer by subtle alterations in balance. Balance is changed by slight movements of the rider's body or by undulations of the road. Lean to the left and the bike will go to the left. So, you must become one with the bike. Sounds really spiritual doesn't it? Handling, after a short period time, becomes second nature and an unconscious act. Basically the bike ends up going about wherever the rider "thinks." The rider actually leans into the turn rather than steering into the turn. Actually a good turn at speed can be achieved by a quick and very slight flip of the bars in the opposite direction of the proposed turn.

That little movement alters the balance perfectly to lean the bike with rider into a very fast turn.

One thing I learned by reading the legendary cycling coach of the '80s; Edward Borysewicz (Eddie "B") is that the bike goes where the rider looks. He coached the concept of looking where you want to be. That kind of goes along with being one with the bike doesn't it? If you want to get around a corner, look at the exit of the corner. The bike will follow your line of sight. If you want to avoid hitting that pothole, resist the temptation to look at the pothole. If you do, chances are that you will guide yourself straight into it. Keep looking at the pothole and you may have the opportunity to buy a brand new alloy wheel.

If you do much group riding with experienced riders you will hear "HOLD YOUR LINE!" from time to time. That is a rider gently encouraging—in biker-Christian love—to ride in a straight, predictable line and at a relatively consistent speed. Not doing so creates a real and present danger to all that follow.

Actually that principle, for me, goes back to my high school driver's education classes. We were taught in order to keep the car traveling in a smooth, straight line to look as far up the road as possible. It works. Erratic drivers (and riders) are most often concentrating on the road only a few feet or less in front. The car will wonder down the road but not in a very straight path.

Looking as far down the road as possible will not only keep you on a straighter, smoother course, it will enable you to see dangers long before they are a crisis. It gives you the ability to be precautionary rather than reactionary. You will begin to see the car approaching from a side road or the guy coming toward you and preparing for a left turn in front of you. I ride on hilly, curvy roads for the most part and I have learned to watch for oncoming vehicles while listening for vehicles approaching from behind. I'd hate to guess how many times I signal the car behind to wait and avoid a head-on. Well, actually it is self-defense. Given the choice, a driver will force a cyclist off the road rather than trade grillwork with that oncoming dump truck.

I've learned another interesting skill out on the road and that is the Law of Peripheral Vision Attention (PVA). I just made up that term, but it sounds really intelligent doesn't it? Vision is best, I'm told, in the center of the field of sight. That makes perfect sense. We see most clearly when looking directly at something. What's interesting is that, and again I'm told, movement is best perceived from the areas of peripheral vision. In other words, we tend to notice *movement* more readily when things move slightly in the edges of our sight line rather than directly in the line of vision. It's what keeps us from being blindsided all the time. Okay, it's what *reduces* me from being blindsided *all* the time. Couple that little gem of knowledge with your new skill of looking way, way down the road and you will be better prepared to react to ever-changing traffic conditions. Please understand that I am talking about movement perception, not clear image identification. And, I'm not talking about the extreme limits of peripheral vision but the just-out-of-the center-of-view peripheral

Now, put this new skill to work in a group ride and you will be more comfortable riding beside a friend. You can keep your primary line of sight down the road and still sense your proximity and position to your friend with your peripheral vision without actually turning every couple of seconds to look. "Uh, pal, you're getting a little too close now." Watch a bike race and you will notice that the racers can ride at high speeds in tight packs and maneuver technical corners without looking directly at each competing rider. It's Peripheral Vision Attention, PVA, and a sense of where everyone should be.

Back a few years ago a well-experienced, local cyclist had a tragic accident on a wide-open road on a clear morning. The wide, two-lane highway had a good, smooth, paved shoulder. A truck loaded with a piece of heavy construction equipment, for whatever reason, was parked well off the highway on the shoulder. The rider, who was extremely familiar with that road, pedaled headlong into the parked truck. All indications were that he made no attempt to avert the obstacle or even to slow. From his point of impact it was unlikely that any other vehicle was involved. Very tragically, the man did not survive the impact. Chances are, he didn't even see the monstrous yellow rig. No one will ever know exactly what happened. But, my theory has always been that his concentration was pointed way up the road. He never expected to see an obstacle in what had always been (and should have been) a clear stretch of highway. The truck was not moving, and more importantly it was not in his peripheral vision. He, subconsciously, was conditioned to see potential danger from the edge of his vision. That stationary truck, big and yellow, didn't register. Lesson? Look up the road *and* scan: keep your eyes moving slightly across the scene ahead. Give your peripheral vision a chance to work.

Once you have gained good handling skills you will feel confident to ride closely in a group. Riding in a group is not only enjoyable, but it is efficient too. We share a physical law for conserving energy with motor racing, speed skating, and freight trains that is often called drafting. We cyclists call it pacelining, but the concept is the same. The idea is to ride closely and directly behind the vehicle ahead to avoid the full impact of air resistance. You see, the rider (skater, freight train, car, or whatever) in front takes the full impact of pushing its way through the air. You and I, being much more clever, hide in the "draft" directly behind another rider where the air resistance is much less. The benefit to a cyclist is as much as thirty percent less energy needed to maintain the same speed. THIRTY PERCENT! Watch a race and you will see pacelining at its best. A group of experienced riders will move along at speeds much higher and for greater distances than a single rider can maintain alone. It's a pleasure to ride with group of riders who know how to work a line. The lead rider should stay on the front (on the "pull") for only a few seconds and then gradually move to the leeward side of the line (get off the "pull") and gently fall back to the rear where he joins the paceline again and takes advantage of a well-deserved rest. The next rider to take the pull fights the tendency to raise the speed and maintains a constant pace. He or she takes the pull for just a few seconds and the

SADDLE SORE SPIRITUALITY

whole cycle repeats over and over again. Imagine going faster and longer than you can by yourself while using thirty percent less energy. Try it.

Pacelining has its own built-in problem though. Remember that premise that we go where we are looking? In a paceline or in a tight group all you see is the rider directly in front. That may be great for drafting, but now your vision is about two and a half feet up the road. Pop Quiz:

If all you see is the Snickers Bar in a jersey pocket of the rider just in front of you, where are you going?

A. To a second place finish.
B. To the first convenience store to get your own Snickers.
C. Anywhere the rider in front of you goes.
D. All of the above.

(Answer: D)

Well, I suppose the *best* answer may be "Anywhere the rider if front of you goes." But, the other answers may be very true too. That's where your vision, and therefore your attention, is. Now, since you are so concentrated on that Snickers Bar, where ever that goes so go you.

If he (or she) gets to the finish line first, you just got second place. Was that why you spent all those hours and miles in training: second? If the lead group crashes, guess who is on top of the carnage? Well, I suppose those other bodies do create a cushion effect for the inevitable contact with the pavement. I have seen it many, many times when someone crashes out, several riders pile on like Pop Warner kids in a tackling drill. I was in a criterium race in Florida several years ago when someone near the lead misjudged a left turn on the first lap. He went down and when I got to the corner it was blocked with riders checking for road rash. I think I was the only one in the field to avoid a close encounter of the asphalt kind. Why? Because I read Eddie B's book and I was looking at the exit of the turn: not the pack immediately in front of me. And with my Peripheral Vision Attention (PVA) I was alerted to the disaster in time to avoid being the disaster. I didn't follow all the others into the pile of bikes and bandages. I was concentrating on where I *wanted* to be rather than where I was at the moment. I finished second in that race because of a different stupid move that we won't talk about. Cycle racing is such a brainy sport.

So where do we keep our vision in a paceline or in a group? It's hard to ride in that draft and still be able to see. I often try to sit up high enough to be able to see slightly over the shoulder of the rider in front of me. Sometimes I will ride just slightly to one side: usually opposite the direction of the wind. I would rather sacrifice a little draft advantage than ride blind. If nothing else, I will peek around the person in front every few moments and duck back into the tunnel. In reality, roads are not generally dead straight for long, and pacelines are not arrow true either.

Shadows are a great key point to watch too depending on the direction of the sunlight. As long as the sun is casting a shadow to one side or the other the riders' shadows can tell you volumes. They can indicate how close or far apart the riders up front are from each other. They can tell you when someone goes out of position to avoid an obstacle in the road. Be careful of the shadows though (that sounds like a movie promo). You can get dazed sort of like watching the wheel in front of you and miss seeing the 20-ton dump truck coming in your lane. And, of course, riders' shadows are no good when riding directly into or away from the sun. This shadow watching thing must have some deep spiritual parallel like the right path being revealed from the light casting in the darkness. Oh I don't know. I've spent hours trying to figure that one out. Can anyone offer any good suggestions?

So, keeping your head up and your focus up the road is easier than you may imagine. It's just a matter of forming the habit. By keeping my vision up the road I can avoid crashes, potholes, unpredictable fellow riders, dogs, and trash. I can see where the corners are and what the condition of the road is ahead.

Cycling has a certain protocol in paceline and group riding too. All the riders absolutely must communicate with one another. The rider on the pull (the one in the lead position taking all that wind in the chest) not only has the most work to do, but also has the solemn responsibility to scan the road for danger and warn the other riders. Bumps, potholes, and gravel in the road must be seen and the warning given to riders behind. Information like "CAR UP!" (A car is approaching), "CAR RIGHT! or LEFT!" (Yep, a car is approaching from the side), or "DOG LEFT/RIGHT!!!!! must be shouted to the following riders and then relayed along the paceline so everyone knows what to expect. The DOG alert is extremely important.

The last rider in the line has a job too, other than resting for a few moments. That rider must be vigilant for cars approaching from behind and pass that information up the line as well. When the rider on the pull decides to get off the pull it is good to know that good Ol' Bubba Junior isn't coming around in his '67 Dodge pick-up at 70 mile per hour. Junior thinks cyclists are on the road purely for his juvenile enjoyment.

Wow! Let's recap.

- Look where you want to be, not where you are.
- Keep your focus as far up the road as you can: it keeps you straight and gives you early warnings of danger.
- Danger coming at you from the side is best brought to your awareness if you keep your sight on the goal ahead.
- Don't focus your attention on the person directly in front of you; you will follow that person into whatever problems they encounter. You won't see disaster coming.
- Paceline. If the group works together, all members will be more efficient than any one member riding alone. Each member takes the stress of the air resistance, but only for a short time. The group can ride faster and longer than any one rider.
- Riding with a group has an obligation to take a turn in the front, to warn of obstacles and danger, and to pass the word.

"♪Turn your eyes upon Jesus. Look full in His wonder face. And the things of earth will grow strangely dim...in the sight of His glory and grace.♪" I have wonderful memories of that great old hymn going back to my very young days in the First Baptist Church of Mishawaka, Indiana. I can still vividly picture in my mind singing that song and gazing up at the image of Jesus in those magnificent stained glass windows. Its message humbles me still today just as much as it did as a child all those years ago.

So how do we keep our Christian life on course? The scriptures keep telling us to keep our focus—our spiritual sight—on the goal we are striving to attain: eternity with our wonderful Lord. If we keep our focus on the day-to-day problems we encounter we will be drawn into the potholes and dangers of life. If you want to end up in divorce for instance, keep your attention focused on marital problems. If you have your attention on finances, how do you expect to see the blessings that God has for you? That far-sightedness keeps us from wavering and wandering from side to side. It keeps us from making our spiritual journey a danger to others. HOLD YOUR LINE!

Keeping your eyes upon the Lord and all of HIS glory makes us more aware of the dangers that can come from the side: from areas in our life where we never expected to see problems. You see, by focusing in on GOD, HE increases our Spiritual Peripheral Vision (SPVA). (I know; I made that up too, but it does sound theological doesn't it?) HE sharpens our spirits with discernment so that we are aware of the danger to our spiritual life and are able to avoid disaster. How many humble Christians have been terribly wounded by ministers caught in sin? Where was their focus: on the pulpit or on the cross beyond it?

God seemed to have placed my wife and I in a series of churches and ministries a few years ago in which pastors, ministers, and church leaders failed. Seeing your pastor on the front page of the Saturday morning newspaper in handcuffs being led away by federal agents is tough to accept. CRASH, we didn't see that one coming! God's SPVA prepared us for that. In another church not too many months later our faith was not shaken when a fine lady of the congregation announced after Sunday morning altar call that she had to confess to an affair with the pastor. Okay. But, several other women stood up and sort of said something like "You too?" God had prepared us to not look to the spiritual Snickers bar in the pastor's back jersey pocket, but to the Lord God on high. Many of the congregation suffered terrible spiritual wounds: Roman road rash. They got blindsided. They had their sight fixed on the pulpit not on the cross. Many, I suspect carry the scars of that disaster today.

Danger in our spiritual lives, those things that will make us waver on our journey to a righteous life and Heaven, can be detected before they hit us if we are aware of that SPVA. Often turmoil does not come from directly in line with our spiritual objectives. It comes from little temptations, disappointments, doubts and other things we just often don't pay attention to. So, we don't respond to those very faint signals and get blindsided by the deacon's affair with the organist or the lack of offering for the mission trip or the poor attendance at the special prayer meeting. We had our spiritual attention directed straight ahead looking for satan to attack in full red suit spewing fire and hitting us with some strange, unexplainable disease. We are prepared for that.

What is that Spiritual Peripheral Vision Attention and how do we use it? It is many things I think, but primarily it is discernment. How many Christians have you known who seemingly know what is the correct or maybe the incorrect path to follow? Maybe they did not know exactly what was wrong with that music and worship minister candidate the selection board was recommending, but they knew he was not the man for the job. Who was not surprised when he brought the rock band in to replace the choir?

How do we gain Spiritual Peripheral Vision

Attention—uh, discernment? First of all we have to pay attention to what the Holy Spirit is telling us. To know what the Holy Spirit is saying we have to maintain dialogue with Him. We can't ignore Him on a day-to-day basis and expect to hear Him clearly when danger hovers. Pay attention to the Holy Spirit's voice so that you will know it clearly whenever He speaks. He has a gentle voice that may be drowned out by the turmoil if we are not tuned to know it. Before I was sent to Red Beach in Viet Nam in 1967 I paid little attention to sirens unless they were directly behind my car and accompanied by flashing lights. You see I was used to city sounds, and sirens were just background noise: a part of the landscape. But, on Red Beach, a siren meant we were being attacked! I got to the point I could hear the siren's very first note long before it gained enough volume to actually be an alert. I could be in the mortar hole before it reached full pitch. To this day I can hear an emergency vehicle before anyone else. And, I still pay close attention to its warning.

We have to know the instruction book: the Bible. We have to know the Word to know when that visiting preacher is spewing out wrong doctrine. If it doesn't match up with the scriptures, you are about to have a problem coming at you from the blind side.

We have to stay in prayer. Keep asking God for wisdom, knowledge, and discernment. In other words, keep your sight on your goal, but pay attention to movement and voices around you.

Spiritual pacelining works too. We can lead a spiritual life by struggling against sin and satan alone. But, using the help of Godly friends will make it much, much easier and more successful. Not only that, but your assistance will help them too. The group can attain more and attain it more efficiently than each member working alone. So, surround yourself with those who have the same goals and values as you.

Now that you are part of that hard charging and soul saving group of believers, understand that obstacles will still pop up in your blessed path. You have the same obligation to scan for danger and pass the word to others. "BAD DOCTRINE AHEAD!" "TEMPTATION RIGHT!" Now the church can really travel!

Part of that benefit to sit in the paceline is the obligation to take your turn at the front and face the pressure of the world's resistance. If you don't step out and exercise your spiritual strength you will overload the rest of the group. When the time comes when you *must* pull for yourself, you may not be strong enough to do it. You may change the pace and drop the rest of the group.

On the other hand, don't try to stay in the front all of the time. You will burn all of your energy and fail. Even when you do take your turn in the back to rest, you may not have enough strength to hang on. You all have to take your turn both on the pull and on the back in order to maintain the pace of the group. I know you can cite ministers and members who seem to always be taking the lead role. Many pastors have been in their pulpits for a lifetime. But, I venture that you will find they ride with another group as well as their own congregation. If not, take note of how successful their churches are. Are they moving spiritually faster and using less energy than they could alone?

Wow! Let's recap.

- Look where you want to be, not where you are.
- Keep your focus as far up the road of your spiritual life as you can: it keeps you straight and gives you early warnings of danger.
- Danger coming at you from the side is best brought to your awareness if you keep your sight on the goal ahead and scan the future.
- Don't focus your attention on the person directly in front of you; you will follow

- that person into whatever problems they encounter. You won't see disaster coming.
- Paceline. If the group works together, all members will be more efficient than any one member riding alone. Each member takes the stress of the world's resistance, but only for a limited time. The group can live better and happier than any one member.
- Riding with a group has an obligation to take a turn in the front, to warn of obstacles and danger, and to pass the word.

♪Keep your eyes upon Jesus.... ♪

Chapter 6

CAPTAINS AND SEAMEN

This year's racing season is in full gear and I find myself searching the web several times a day scanning for news and results from the races around the world. I attempt to either watch first hand or record the weekly cycle racing coverage on that not-indoor-sports network: you know the one that airs the Tour De France every year. Since they usually air the racing segments on Sunday afternoons I am often unable to view them live. So, I normally attempt to record the program and watch it later in the evening. I say "attempt" because although I do actually understand how to set the program recording function, I somehow manage to record something entirely different. I amaze myself at how often I enter the wrong time, day, or channel. This is not the fault of the recording device, it is operator error. Of course

I don't discover that until I have settled into the recliner with iced soda and chips beside me and prepared for an evening of cycling drama. On it comes: not the Tour De Whatever, but maybe the tenth rerun of a "Cops" episode or "The Best of The NCAA Playoffs: 1959." My wonderful wife who is not that thrilled by cycling on TV is on the sofa reading and ever so stealthily glancing at the TV. She is so kind as not to ask. I end up settling for "Law and Order" and re-recording the race from the Wednesday rerun program. It's become a tradition.

The other thing I do during the race season is share my enthusiasm with anyone who will listen and with many who don't care. They are really nice: most don't tell me to go get a life. To the untrained eye, cycle racing can be just plain boring. It's sort of like watching hockey on TV. It looks like lots of uncontrolled agony with the occasional thrill of a goal being scored. I really do understand that hockey is a very intellectual sport. The big difference in cycle racing is that we only have one goal and it's at the very end: or so it seems. We don't have many fights, but I suppose the occasional crash makes up for that. I have a friend who loves hockey and tries to explain it to me. He patiently listens to my discourse on cycling. We considerately respect each other's domain and genuinely fake interest.

Cycle racing is a fascinating sport. People are intrigued to learn that it is in fact a team sport. Yes, a team sport. Okay, Roller Derby is a team sport on wheels too, but nothing like cycling. At first glance it appears to be every rider for him, or herself. Not so if it is done right. And, as physically demanding as cycling is, it is guided by constant, profound and detailed strategy. You see, the winner is not only the strongest rider but the strongest rider on the strongest—and smartest—team.

A racing team is built of riders who possess certain attributes. Riders are chosen based on their skill and the race they will be challenging. Some are sprinters. Some are time trial specialists. Some are climbers—mountain goats. Some are just plain road soldiers. They are there to do anything demanded of them. They are quite expendable and will sacrifice themselves without hesitation for the good of the team.

Each team has a captain. The Captain is the designated leader of the team and expected race winner. The team is dedicated to supporting their Captain to the demise of all other team members. You see, any one rider is probably incapable of maintaining dominance throughout an entire stage race. The team as a whole if choreographed together can launch their captain, and their team, to triumph. Now don't get the wrong idea, the captain can't just sit back and wait to be towed across the finish line without contributing to the effort. He directs the strategy and he must be strong enough to continue the assault once the rest of the team has done their part.

I guess at this point I need to explain the different type of races in cycling, because the type of race will dictate the skills the various riders must have. Perhaps I should devote a chapter to this. You see—and this is another reason cycling is so appealing to so many people—racing is so diverse that it can satisfy the interest of a variety of personalities. Cycle racing can be a short individual time trial or a three week epic stage race around an entire country. It can be done inside on a closed, banked track or on open roads.

The preferred race in American racing is the criterium or the "crit." It is a short, fast race usually on closed off streets. The course is generally about a one mile loop that is designed to be "technical": lots of turns and tight spots that require precise bike handling skills as well as speed. Riders will race for a specified number of laps or perhaps for a certain amount of time (say thirty minutes) plus something like five laps. Crits are exciting to be in and exciting to watch. Since they are staged on short loops the crowd gets to see the action up close and personal every few seconds. Since they are designed with lots of tight turns and the riders are usually grouped tightly together, they get to see action every few seconds also.

The road race is more popular in Europe but is now gaining popularity in the United States as well. Like its name implies, it is staged out on open roads. Road race courses generally are set up between about fifty and about one hundred miles: sometimes more, rarely less. Since they are so long the group of riders called the peloton—oh the French, why can't they just call it the group of riders—may spread out along the course. Riders then are not bunched up so much like they are in a crit, and the courses are not so tight and technical. And, since it is staged out on the open road the terrain changes constantly. A road race may have miles of flat, steady roads followed by monster climbs followed by white-knuckle descents back into the valley. The course may be open to automobile traffic or in the case of major road races closed to all but bikes and team cars. The open-to-traffic courses present their own special excitement.

Stage races combine different styles of events into several days of racing but generally are set in the road race style. Each day's event is a stage. Stage races may incorporate road races, time trials, and occasionally even crits. Each day, or stage, is a race within a race. Each stage has a winner for that segment. Every racer's elapsed time for each stage is kept and an ongoing total time is figured for each rider for the whole event. The leader is the guy or girl with the least total elapsed time regardless how he or she has placed in any individual stage. So you can see that a stage race winner does not need to win any individual stage: it's the total time over the entire set of stages that counts. The most consistent rider over the several days has the best chance of winning. Stage races can range from a weekend event to something like the Tour De France occupying three weeks in July, circling the country, and covering well over 2,000 miles. Hundreds of thousands of people line the routes of some of these events. Millions watch on TV. That sort of makes the Super Bowl seem a bit less spectacular doesn't it?

The time trial is a unique race. Sometimes called the "Race of Truth," it places riders on a course all alone and timed for the entire course. The rider is only racing against the clock. For the individual time trial no team is there to help and no peloton is there to judge performance against. It's just the bike, the rider, the course, and the clock. You may understand why it's called the

SADDLE SORE SPIRITUALITY

Race of Truth. Occasionally a stage race will incorporate a team time trial where the members of each team ride the time trial course together. The time for the team is taken when the fifth rider of the team crosses the finish line. That takes a great deal of skill and practice. It looks ever so easy; but believe me, it's not. Riding a seamless paceline in perfect unison at absolute top speed within inches of the wheel in front takes skill, practice, trust, and absolute concentration. Members and fans of the Seven-11 team can vouch for that. When they were relatively new to European racing and fielding an all-American team in the Tour De France, they faced a crucial team time trial stage. Now these were all highly experienced professional cyclists who were proud to represent America in a European dominated sport. Their effort was a disaster from the starter's countdown and it went downhill from there. Instead of a beautiful and artful dance of speed, it looked more like the Keystone Cops meet Rocky Balboa. What a catastrophe. Bob Roll, who was on that team, still recalls with laughter how terrible that day was.

Track racing is an interesting, exciting, and unique style of racing. It is done on a very short, very high-banked oval track—a velodrome. It's the cycle racing you see most often at the Olympic

Games: you know—the events that no one really seems to understand what is going on except the guys actually on the track and, they even seem a trifle confused most of the time too. They seem to spend most of the race riding slowly, sitting still and sometimes start on opposite sides of the track from the competition. I won't get into the reasoning of starting on opposite sides, but suffice it to say sitting still is a masterful strategy. Think of it this way: the race is won on the last lap, not the first lap. Why waste all that energy getting to the finish when all you have to do is wait out the other guy and dash for the win? Oh yes, we do have the two guys racing each other from opposite sides of the track. I must admit that appears just a little snobbish. However in today's enlightened world, it may be politically correct.

Most of the more interesting track races are not seen at the Olympics though. The Olympic crowd is not amused by really fun racing. Go to a local velodrome on a Friday night and you may see a keirin which sort of looks like everyone trying to catch a moped. The guy on the moped has the Snickers. You may see a Madison or maybe a team event where riders swing each other in and out of competition sort of like team speed skating.

I especially like the win-and-out event. After a fair warm-up period the bell sounds and the winner of the next lap is the race winner. Oh, it doesn't stop there. Each successive lap is a sprint for the next placing: second, third, fourth and so on. By the time the last three or four guys are left on the track struggling for a meaningless position, it becomes a matter of shear survival. Every lap is an all out sprint. The strategy is to calculate who you can outsprint on which lap. Go too soon and you are toast: go too late and you lose a placing.

A sister event to the win-and-out is the devil-takes-the-hindermost. It's sort of the opposite of the win-and-out. After the warm-up and the bell, the last guy to cross the line—the hindermost—is eliminated. The next lap is the same with the last guy over the line being eliminated. The finishing positions are earned from last to first: backwards from most race events. That continues until all but one is eliminated. It's sort of a last man standing event. Imagine the strategy in that. The skill is to sprint fast enough on each lap to avoid elimination but not enough to expend too much energy. The whole pack is nipping at your heels like a pack of dogs before breakfast. The weakest riders give all they have each lap and force the stronger riders to use up precious energy before the last two remain.

Some of the unique races aside, track racing can be awesome and difficult to the extreme. It is great to watch too, since it is done on a very short track and the spectators are virtually on top of the action.

When I was stationed in San Diego, I used to go to the velodrome in Balboa Park on Friday nights. It was more exciting than the fist fights at a NASCAR event. One time I took a shipmate of mine who went along out of shear boredom and partially just to be nice to me. His idea of exercise was a nice walk around Shoney's salad bar. But, after the first Friday night, he was hooked! He loved it.

Balboa Velodrome was open to the public whenever it was not being used for race events. Anyone could go in and practice or just try out the track. I did. I can tell you from firsthand experience that riding on a high-bank track is not easy. You see, those banks are much steeper than they look. The natural tendency of a rider is to ride upright with the bike straight up and down. Well, on the very first lap I learned that the banking is so steep that the uphill pedal will clip the track unless the bike is leaned over hard and pushing into the curve. I also learned that it is a far greater falling distance if one falls *down* the bank than if one falls *up* the bank. Falling on the down side of the bank hurts exponentially more than falling to the up-bank side. Now, the physics

SADDLE SORE SPIRITUALITY

law that governs falling on velodrome tracks is that no one *ever* falls UP! On my second try I learned that in order to keep the bike at a safe angle relative to the banking of the track I had to muscle up some significant speed. Otherwise the bike wants to position itself vertical to the earth, not the bank of the track. Darn, clipped a pedal again! The real track racers do all this with fixed gear bikes and no brakes. I learned on that first attempt at velodrome riding to stay way down on the warm-up strip at the bottom of the track. That's equivalent to skiing on the kiddies bunny slope. I don't track race.

Back to team racing. The average run of the mill road race or crit will have various obstacles included in the course meant to sadistically eliminate all but the strongest riders. Those obstacles may be hills, mountains, fast drops off of mountains, long and fast flat sections, tight and curvy technical sections, and so on. The famed Paris-Roubaix (*l'enfer du Nord*, or the *Hell of the North*) is one of the premier one-day classics that runs at least in part along roads that the Romans built. The Romans used large cobblestones and as you may imagine these roads were not silky smooth to begin with and are now in need of some significant repair. Of course the race is traditionally run in the spring when rain is likely. So, the

Paris-Roubaix is unique in its demands. Just to finish is an accomplishment. Teams have been known to offer bonuses to riders who simply finish. Riders have been known to fake mechanical problems just to abandon with some sort of pride.

I said earlier that the team captain can't be expected to excel all the time at every aspect of a long road race. That's where the team comes in. Each team member has specific talents and skills. On the mountain stages, the teams have climbing specialists. On the flat, fast stages teams have sprinters. They are the riders who can finish the last three hundred or so meters of the stage with a blistering 40 miles per hour (and more) insane dash to the finish line. Some are simply all-around workhorses who can do a little bit of everything.

So how does this help the team leader? For one thing, the team does all the heavy work before the captain needs to take over. Remember when we discussed the advantage of riding a paceline? The team will take the brunt of the wind and allow the captain to sit in the back of the group so that he, or she, can save energy for when it's needed most. They also surround their captain when the peloton is riding close together and roads are narrow in order to protect him from crashes and injury.

SADDLE SORE SPIRITUALITY

Climbing specialists, mountain goats, will lead the captain up the slopes. This may sound a little odd and you may be thinking the climb is as tough for two as it is for one: not much aerodynamic advantage at six miles per hour. Well, yes. But the advantage of having one of your own along to focus on and encourage you is astonishing. That goes for any riding. I always climb harder and faster on a club ride than I do by myself. It's a matter of pride. I'm not about to let my weaknesses be seen. And, yes there is a drafting benefit even at slow speeds. Every little bit of assistance helps. On especially hard mountainous courses teams may have two or three climbers. When one exhausts, another will take over the pull until the only one left is the captain who wins the stage and gets all the glory. UGH!

Sprinters are interesting riders. On long, flat stages of road races the peloton generally stays together. The course provides little opportunity for a small group to split itself from the pack: a break away. So the last three hundred meters or so belong to the sprinters. They tag along at the back of the peloton all day so that they can be fresh and in position for that final few seconds of controlled mayhem. The sprint starts two or three kilometers from the finish with the speed ratcheting up and the sprinters jockeying for position.

CAPTAINS AND SEAMEN

Sprinters have their own road soldiers too: lead-out men. These are sort of second string sprinters who boost up the speed of the sprint and allow their teammate to follow behind in the slipstream. They bring the speed up as much as possible and guide their man through the traffic of contestants until they are completely exhausted and skillfully relinquish position to their designated sprinter. The sprinter slingshots around and wins the stage, gets all the glory, and the girl. UGH!

Sprinters are specialists and rarely have a chance to win the overall stage race. They cherish winning individual stages. In many cases, sprinters don't even finish a long and grueling stage race. Often they abandon on the mountain stages.

So, if the sprinters don't have much influence on the overall outcome of a stage race and they sit back on the flat stages and they can't climb, what good are they to the team? They bring a victory to the team. A win is a win is a win. Teams are put together and funded by corporate sponsors, and the team along with its sponsors gets all the publicity for a sprint win. Fast, sprint finishes are among the most exciting moments in cycling and therefore get the most publicity.

Every team has some riders who actually excel at nothing in particular. They are simply all-around good, strong riders who can do whatever is demanded of them. These riders are called domestiques. In French it literally translates as "servant." These riders are the servants to the team. They protect the star riders by being on the front and taking all the wind resistance in a paceline. They are also quite literally water carriers going back to the team support cars and packing as many water bottles as they can carry to deliver up the road to the rest of the team. They carry food and medical supplies as well. When called upon, they chase down breakaways to prevent some other team from getting a significant lead on the peloton. When a team leader or some other important team member crashes, flats, or has some other mechanical problem and the support car is not close enough to help, a domestique will willingly give up his bicycle if necessary to keep his leader in competition. If the team leader falls back for some reason, the domestique will pace him back up to the peloton and back into competition. Rarely do they get any recognition and rarely do they finish anywhere but in the rear of the race. They exhaust themselves for the benefit of their leaders.

Good specialists and domestiques push the competition as well as assisting their captain. Since their purpose is not so much to win as to work for their team; they can, and do, attack and force the competitors to chase and expend huge amounts of energy. A good mountain goat will attack off the front and force other teams and other captains to counter attack.

Allowing a rogue rider to gain too much time on a single stage can disrupt the strategy of the entire race. Domestiques often attempt a small break away on relatively flat stages in hopes of sneaking away and gaining precious publicity from a stage win. These breaks seldom work, but they do cause the rest of the teams to have to chase them down and, again, use precious energy.

So, if the team is made up of all these specialists, where does that leave the captain: sounds like he is getting a free ride to the winner's platform? Well, the captain has to be the rider who is able to take over where the specialists leave off. The greatest climber in the world is of no use if the captain can't continue the attack when the specialist exhausts. His lieutenants can only support him so much and he must be able to carry on from there. He has to be able to use the advantage of having been sitting in the protection of the pack when he is called upon to prove himself. He has to be able to finish those dizzying climbs when his teammates have given all the legs they have to give. Most importantly he must be a master on-the-road tactician and strategist. He has to be

SADDLE SORE SPIRITUALITY

able to read the race and know when to attack and when to rest his team. He has to know who is a threat and who is an interloper. He has to know how to best use the terrain and the race conditions to keep his team and himself in position to win. He has to be the strongest all around rider on the team. He has to be able to sprint fast enough to maintain a front-of-the-pack position on the flats. He has to be a strong enough climber to be capable of finishing with the most powerful climbers. He has to be a dynamic leader in order to direct the rest of the team while reading the course and the competition. Think about it, sitting in the protection of team mates and having others take the brunt of the wind and competition may not be as easy as it sounds. After all, the captain has to keep up the pace along with everyone else and then must be strong enough to continue the attack and finish the victory. Remember, his team mates are pushing the attack on the competition, and the leader must be right there with them in order to be in position to finish off the win.

Teams need one leader. Lieutenants and domestiques must know precisely who they are sacrificing for. In 1985 Greg LeMond was riding his second Tour De France on the la Vie Claire team along with team leader and cycling legend Bernard Hinault. Hinault had crashed and was suffering badly from injuries. LeMond had the opportunity to attack and win the Tour; but he was ordered to sit back and wait for his captain, Hinault. The rest of the team would not support LeMond's attacks, choosing to be loyal to the designated captain. LeMond finished second behind a victorious Hinault.

In the 1986 Tour De France, Hinault promised to ride for and support LeMond as a reward for his loyalty in the '85 race. Hinault, the five-time Tour winner, seemed to renege on his promise and attacked LeMond at crucial stages. LeMond demanded his position as captain as he had been promised and in doing so spilt the loyalty of the rest of the team. At that point LeMond's leadership and determination took over and he won the full support of his team along with the race itself.

More recently team management of several prestigious teams have attempted to compete without a declared, specific team captain due to the absence of former leaders from either retirement or disqualification. Some managers have chosen to try and support two or three possible leaders and see which one is the best leader. Other managers have chosen to wait until a leader emerges on the road and then throw the support of the team to that rider. Neither strategy has been successful.

Team techniques are beneficial not only in racing situations but in every day group rides too. I fully understand that the Saturday morning club ride is not a race. It is a recreational outing meant to bring cyclists together in a sort of on-the-road mobile social gathering. You know, let's all ride a relaxed pace and have a good conversation while admiring the wild flowers along the country roadway. In practice, a couple of interesting things happen. Certain riders seem to take on the roll of whatever their forte happens to be: domestique, climber, sprinter, team mom. In most cases the riders filter into position without realizing that they even have a forte and that they are actually exercising it. Secondly, everyone surreptitiously exhibits a natural inclination to compete.

The most noticeable is the rider who likes to stay on the pull: ride out in front of the group while everyone else sits in the slipstream. Good group technique suggests that one should stay on the pull for only a short time: maybe a couple of minutes. Staying out too long defeats the purpose. However, most groups will have a rider or two who love to pull for, what seems like, the entire ride. Does that sound like a domestique type to you? Now, chances are very slim that you will be able to cast me in that role. In fact, if you find me on the pull for more than a two or three minutes it was purely by mistake. I think I am old enough to deserve a place in the back of the pack. I've earned it. If I stay out front too long I get queasy and disoriented.

Groups generate climbing goats also. Give some guys a good hill and they will try their best to beat everyone to the crest. Cyclists have this special portion of the brain that makes all hills appear to be legendary Alps peaks and all group rides take on the form of a pro peloton. So why not just let them go? I read the story of the tortoise and the hare. The tortoise wins. Well, that same portion of the brain won't allow us to be embarrassed. So the natural climbing ace serves to inspire everyone else to do their very best on the incline. Guess what? By pushing yourself to match the climbing ace, you are gaining strength and becoming a better climber yourself. We all do much better when we try and match someone just a little faster. One day you will be encouraging some young whipper-snapper to persevere and fly up that hill. By the way, you won't often find me leading anyone up the climbs. I am now, after many years of suffering, old enough to not be humiliated by my struggling ascends. After all, a man my age just getting up the hill is something to admire. It hasn't always been that way.

Group rides generate a leader as well.

Someone will become the on-the-road strategist encouraging weaker riders and guiding the group through obstacles. This may or may not be the designated ride leader. I was on a ride a couple of weeks ago when we came up to a main highway. One guy in the group actually talked the designated ride leader into changing the route because he felt the highway was too dangerous. He was wrong, but he won the debate. What a wimp. He became the leader in practice if not in title. Leaders will be the ones shouting "DOG ON THE RIGHT" and pointing out potholes and trash in the roadway: and changing the route in mid-ride.

Even on recreational rides we cyclists turn on that special section of the brain that makes us uncontrollably competitive. We just simply cannot be shown to be frail. Now, that doesn't mean we are race intensive insane, but we are guarded against being judged as weak. I have started probably hundreds of rides with guys who all agree at the outset that we are going to do a slow, easy ride today. "No hammering!" "Oh no, not me. My legs are toast today. I really need a recovery ride today." Not too long into the ride we are attacking each other like Grant and Lee: so much for a rest and recovery ride. In cycling there is a phenomenon called half-wheeling. I'm not sure, but I think it is uncontrollable. It starts off as a slow, easy, conversational ride with two riders riding along side by side. As they leisurely soft-pedal and discuss tomorrow's Sunday School lesson one rider's front wheel eases just a little ahead of the other; maybe half a wheel. Well, not to be seen as a slacker, the other rider picks up the pace just enough to keep even. Keeping even is hard to do, so our second rider unintentionally creeps half-a-wheel ahead of his friend. And, not to hold his friend back, our first rider pushes up even himself. Remember what "even" means? It ends up being a half wheel ahead. Now, imagine this going on for four or five miles and before anyone realizes it our leisurely riders are passing eighteen wheelers and accelerating away. By the end of the ride both riders collapse from exhaustion and reminisce about how they were going to have a nice, easy, rest-ride today. It's good training.

So; the bottom line is that when we cycle with others, whether it is group rides, recreational rides, or competitive racing we all have certain skills and abilities that contribute to the group as a whole. Even being the slowest guy in the group can encourage another rider who has been training his brains out and proves that all that effort has paid off. I know that feeling.

God has specialist also. He gave these specialists unique skills to carry out the purpose of the church. These are called the spiritual gifts. Some have the skill, uh gift, of wisdom, some miracles, some healing, some knowledge, some preaching, some teaching and so on and so on. As Paul said to the Ephesians, *"11And he gave some, apostles; and some, prophets; and some, evangelists; and some, pastors and teachers; 12For the perfecting of the saints, for the work of the ministry, for the edifying of the body of Christ: 13Till we all come in the unity of the faith, and of the knowledge of the Son of God, unto a perfect man, unto the measure of the stature of the fulness of Christ:"* Ephesians 4:13. See that part that says "...for the edifying of the body of Christ." We sacrifice and give to the fullest the gifts and skills that God bestowed on us for the good of Christ and His victory: our Captain, our Team.

Everyone in the church—the flesh and blood, everyday walk around church, not the stained glass and steeple building—is an important member of the team. The scriptures call it "the body." Each member has an important role to play in the "...*Edifying of the body...*" A good team needs a diversity of talents and personalities. Without good climbers the team will not bring its captain to the finish at the village in the valley. If the team members get too proud of their individual talents, they stand a good chance of destroying the goal of the team. Paul in another letter told the followers in Corinth, " *¹²For as the body is one, and hath many members, and all the members of that one body, being many, are one body: so also is Christ.*" 1 Corinthians 12:12 Remember our sprinters? Those guys seldom have a chance to win the big prize: the overall stage race. They do have a chance to struggle along on hundred plus mile stages to sprint savagely for the last few meters for perhaps a shot at a single stage win. Remember, many don't even finish the race once it goes into the mountains. Climbing is not their gift. But, the team rejoices and enjoys the stage victory of a single member. Paul continues in 1 Corinthians to say, *"²¹And the eye cannot say unto the hand, I have no need of thee: nor again the head to the feet, I have no need of you. ²²Nay, much more those members of the body, which seem to be more feeble, are necessary:"* 1 Corinthians 12:21-22

What about the domestiques? Oh how precious are those in the Kingdom who work hard every day doing the little things that bring glory to God. The scriptures are full of examples of domestiques (servants) who serve our Lord. Many have been rewarded in Glory. Christ speaks highly of "good and faithful" servants. "The meek shall inherit the earth." Wow! I'll be domestique for Christ for that kind of a victory!

Chapter 7

THE OFF SEASON

The past two weeks have been exceptionally cold for middle Tennessee. It is mid-February, and winter has fully settled in. As I look out my office window I can see thin, green blades of grass peeking up through the shallow snow. They look like masses of little cartoon characters standing on tiptoes trying to escape the icy grip of a full inch of the white incursion. The sun is out now, so the ground will soon return to a brownish green, and the grass blades can relax. Yesterday I spent the day watching out this same window as snowflakes constantly swirled and the sky had a cold, gray, evil look. The temperature stayed in the high twenties and the air whipped around the neighborhood as if looking for warmth itself. The cold and occasional snow dusting has invaded for about three weeks. When the temperature does warm, it brings on a bone-chilling rain. January was unusually warm, so this colder-than-normal February feels even more inconsiderate.

This climate at this time of year is really not optimum for cycling: it's an outdoor activity. I do have a nice attached garage that is good shelter from the elements, and my thoughtful wife bought me a rather nice indoor cycle trainer last Christmas along with a whole library of race videos and training DVDs. I'm probably the only man in the neighborhood with a TV, DVD, VCR mounted beside the workbench. I can put my road bike on the trainer and adjust the resistance from easy spin up to lung busting mountain simulation. I can go along with a group of guys on a training ride in the Rockies without leaving my garage and electric space heater, or I can ride the Tour De France with the best racers in the world. I can even do my own custom spinning class and choose the torture-of-the-day workout from dozens of options. These videos are great! No matter how much or little effort I put into a ride I can't get dropped by the group. I can sit back and relax and still keep up with the group. The ride leader doesn't even grouch at me. Technology is amazing.

Now, I also have all of the cold weather gear for riding outdoors year around. I've got the tights, two-layer gloves, windproof coat, booties to keep the toes from freezing, ear muffs, skull cap, ski mask, and long-sleeve jerseys. I could probably cycle the Iditarod Trail Sled Dog Race with the gear I have. They do have a bicycle version of that race. I absolutely hate to ride in the cold or in the rain. If I do venture out for a winter ride I normally enjoy it once I get past the first ten or fifteen minutes of why-am-I-doing-this misery and cold. Cycling creates its own climate control: exercise induced body heat. The harder one rides, the warmer one gets.

Even with all this high-tech equipment, I usually suffer this time of the year from negative motivation. Okay, the garage is fifty degrees compared to twenty-five outdoors. Fifty degrees and under shelter isn't bad; but sixty-eight and a cushioned, leather desk chair with a window view and a hot cup of tea seems awfully comfortable. I get into a predicament this time of year when I think it's too cold to ride outside and too boring to ride inside. So, I talk myself into not riding at all. "After all, I have a month to six weeks before warm weather and group rides begin." "I can relax today and make up for it tomorrow." "I'll do an extra hard session next time." "It's a long time before I'll be embarrassed for being too fat and riding too slow." I like to use this one best: "Everyone else is **not** training too."

THE OFF SEASON

I forced myself to get on the trainer yesterday. I had been "resting" for six days. That's scriptural isn't it? Oh no, it's work for six days and rest on the seventh. I knew six days had something to do with rest. I also weighed myself. No comment!

I usually back off on my cycling in November and December after a long ten months of hard riding. I just need the rest, and no important events are scheduled that time of year anyway. My motivation is still up, but I relax and only try to keep up enough miles to reach my annual goal. I treat the burnout and give the ol' legs a chance to recover.

January 1 starts my training season. I have a tradition of doing a fifty-mile ride on New Year's day. Icy roads or rain postpone it sometimes, but that's my ritual and I have stuck with it for over twenty years. I also have a written training goal and a diary where I record each mile I pedal. I have daily goals, weekly goals, monthly... and so on. I have specific events that I participate in, and I have training milestones that I establish for those events. Sounds like a plan. The truth is that—and this may be a tradition—by mid-March I am way, way behind on my schedule. The call of the window view has won out over the prospect of cold miles on the road or painful hours on the trainer. Oh, I get motivated again when the

SADDLE SORE SPIRITUALITY

weather warms and daylight savings time arrives. But, March and April are very painful months. If only I had stuck to my plan.... Remember back in Chapter 2 when I advised that the best way to learn and improve was to ride and ride all year? Believe me; I have first-hand, up-front & personal, and face-to-face experience of how hard that is to carry out.

Rest is necessary. Most cycling coaches endorse a program that contains certain days devoted to "active rest." Those days are programmed for easy, relaxed rides: nothing strenuous, but rides non-the-less. Coaches also advise cyclists to plan to peak physically—be at your optimum—for only a few events throughout the season. They find that excelling at every event over a nine-month season is near impossible. At best that approach produces mediocre results across the season.

Too much rest is harmful. The body gets used to a certain physical level of activity and resists when that status quo is challenged. The body cannot gain performance by maintaining a mere preservation level of activity. That concept is active at all levels of performance: not just the couch-potato plateau. I've known cyclists who ride at the same level of difficulty and speed constantly. They may ride quite strongly. But when demanded to excel at the next level—that pack sprint for the city limit sign—they fail. Now some riders are quite content to maintain the level they are at. Maybe some are at their maximum. That's great. But, at some point the body will become so accustomed to that level of activity that it will actually lose conditioning. It finds that it can perform "well enough" on reduced energy. And, of course, the ole brain plays tricks on the ole body. Losses in performance decline so gradually that the change is not even noticed. That's one reason I keep a riding diary. I compare my times and speeds from previous rides. The numbers don't lie. So, in order to maintain, we must challenge ourselves constantly. The degree of challenge depends on the goals you set for yourself. Lance Armstrong put in hundreds, perhaps thousands, of exhausting miles on the slopes of the Alps and the Pyrenees in order to be the best rider in France in July. He did that seven times! "Use it or lose it." He also relaxed after the Tour De France and competed in only select races the remainder of the year. By January he was back in Europe pounding 100-mile training days.

Wow! That was motivating! I'm going to go out for a Sunday afternoon 50-miler. I needed that!

So where are we? Maintaining and improving cycling performance is a matter of balance. No pun intended. Ride too hard and too often and experience burnout and decreased performance. Rest too often or for too long a period; conditioning deteriorates, and motivation declines. Try to dominate every race or event, and prevail at none. The body is damaged by extreme exertion, but it gains when it heals itself during active rest. That's right. ACTIVE rest. The body reacts best, not at total rest, but at a significantly "reduced" activity. So now, when you are having a particularly bad day on the bike, you can tell your riding partners that you are training with "active rest." Boy, I like the way that sounds

Actually; November, December, January, and even February are active training periods for me. They are "active rest" periods. I just don't dare let the "rest" part override the "active" part. If I do, by March the "pain" part overrides the "gain" part.

The cyclist's body is best nurtured not by a steady diet of one level of exertion but by a balanced diet of over exertion, maintenance, active rest, and rest: Balance.

When I was racing (participating in races, let's be honest) I had a specific cyclic training schedule. January and February were devoted to base miles. Just getting the legs used to turning the pedals constantly. In late February through March I increased the miles but incorporated interval training into the routine to get the strength I would need to stay in the race. By April I added one or two sprint sessions into each week's agenda to improve my power at the end of the race.

Throughout the season, I maintained a rounded weekly training program. Monday was an active rest day: an easy "conversation" ride: nothing strenuous. Tuesday was sprint training. Six to ten full power, all-out, 300-meter sprints. Wednesday was a long, steady ride: two to four hours. Thursday was interval training. Intervals are a series of hard, extended power attacks followed by a short recovery period repeated to complete surrender. Friday was a short day, usually a thirty to forty minute time trial. Saturday and Sunday was race day if one was scheduled. If no races were on for a weekend, then it was simulated races with team or group rides.

By October the racing season was over and training reverted back to group rides, maintenance rides, and fun stuff. November and December are too cold to do much of anything, so they became active rest with the emphasis on rest. Two or three days between rides is common for that time of year.

I still maintain that sort of training cycle at a much-reduced intensity even now. I can't let these youngsters think they can dust the old guy ya know. And, I know that if I allow myself to rest too much and for too long I will begin to drastically decline. I don't want to do that. I want to do a 100 mile ride on the day I die from old age: an old, old, old age.

This exertion-rest thing holds at all levels: even on the ride itself. Remember earlier when I was talking about the skill of pace line riding? The rider on the front takes the brunt of the air resistance for a short period of time while the others in the group follow closely in a straight line and "rest" in his or her slipstream. The group can ride faster and further with less energy than each individual can alone.

The Bible is full of examples of work and rest. From the very beginning of scripture Genesis 2:2 tells us *"And on the seventh day God ended his work which he had made; and he rested on the seventh day from all his work which he had made."* God himself rested. Was God resting from the labor of creating the Earth, mankind, all of nature, the entire universe? Or, was he resting in preparation for dealing with sinful man? Both?

> *[1]To every thing there is a season, and a time to every purpose under the heaven: [2]A time to be born, and a time to die; a time to plant, and a time to pluck up that which is planted;*

³A time to kill, and a time to heal; a time to break down, and a time to build up; ⁴A time to weep, and a time to laugh; a time to mourn, and a time to dance; ⁵A time to cast away stones, and a time to gather stones together; a time to embrace, and a time to refrain from embracing; ⁶A time to get, and a time to lose; a time to keep, and a time to cast away; ⁷A time to rend, and a time to sew; a time to keep silence, and a time to speak; ⁸A time to love, and a time to hate; a time of war, and a time of peace. ⁹What profit hath he that worketh in that wherein he laboureth? ¹⁰I have seen the travail, which God hath given to the sons of men to be exercised in it. Ecclesiastes 3:1-10

The book of Mark relates a time in Jesus' ministry after the Disciples had gone through a very trying experience and just before the Feeding of the Five Thousand. Mark 6:31 says, *"And He said unto them, Come ye yourselves apart into a desert place, and rest a while: for there were many coming and going and they had no leisure so much as to eat."*

Throughout the scriptures we are given reference and instruction to fast and pray: to get away from all the stress of our lives and "rest" in Him.

Fasting and praying is a rejuvenating of damaged spiritual muscle. God knows that His mankind cannot fight the fight day in and day out without a season to rest and rebuild. It's like those Monday *easy* rides: the "conversation" rides after an all-out race weekend.

Why is "resting on the Sabbath" so important? If we are living our lives in a sinful world like God would have us live, we will be spiritually exhausted by whatever day you want to call the Sabbath: Sunday. That is the day we recover from the spiritual battles. We let the Lord heal us, rest us, rejuvenate our body and our spirit.

The book of 1Kings chronicles the faithfulness of Elijah and his match with the profits of Baal. Elijah challenged them to a contest to bring fire to their altar. After a day of trying everything they knew to do: nothing. Elijah prepared his altar and sacrifice and doused it three times with water. *"Then the fire of the Lord fell, and consumed the burnt sacrifice, and the wood, and the stones, and the dust, and licked up the water that was in the trench."* 1 Kings 18:38. He then called upon God to bring rain and end a drought in the land. He then had to flee for his life. So he had quite a week. Elijah went into the wilderness and rested after his ordeal and triumph. God gave him food and water and—hmmmmm—rest before he set out on his new job to speak God's word to Israel.

Have you ever known fellow Christians who go hard, spiritually, all the time? You know, the ones who never rest in the Lord or fast and pray. Remember the cyclist who goes all out all the time. He is exerting all the effort he has every day, but his performance is stagnant. Oh, he is propelling down the road, but is he going to win any races? I am concerned with ministers and members who tackle all the jobs all the time. Rest is essential to growth: even spiritually.

How about the church worker who plugs away at the same pace every week: the ones who we can "depend" on. They seem to have set a steady spiritual pace and most likely are not ready to sprint when the demand is set before them. They are wonderful people, but they have not stressed their spiritual muscles enough to tackle the really tough times with confidence. What happens when they find the associate pastor is deep in sin? Do they fall apart or do they have the spiritual stamina to endure? I've seen—and maybe you have too—church members emotionally fall apart when the foundation of their church is attacked.

I sort of like to think of Sunday School as my spiritual rest day. Think about it. In most cases, you are in a class with people who are not going to attack your faith: friends for the most part.

Now the "worldly" folks you deal with all through the week are attacking with vengeance. You get to recover with the Word of God with Godly friends. It's sort of like that conversation intensity Monday ride. Now too, in probably most cases, the average Sunday School lesson is not too exhaustive. Wednesday Bible study, maybe, but usually not Sunday School. It may challenge you to exert your spiritual life next week, but it not too threatening today.

There is a season for riding and a season for training; a season for recovery and a season for discovery. You see, our Father knows that we are best when we practice a balanced life with times of preparation and times of all-out effort. There is a *"Time to rend and a time to sew."* There is a time to lead the mountain climb and a time to sit in the pack. There is a time to lead the (insert the one you are being asked to take over) ministry and a time to be ministered to. I'm not too sure about the *"...a time to speak and a time to be silent."* I really like the *"...a time to rest."*

Are you willing to swallow your athletic pride and take a day or two a week to slow down and do an active rest workout? Are you willing to take a season—a couple of months—and ride like you don't have anything to prove? I know I am. But, then are you willing to use that rest, when the time comes, to go to greater distances, speeds, and heights than you have ever before? That's a little harder phase to move into.

Now, are you willing to go to the desert and rest before you have to feed the five thousand? Are you willing to step back sometimes and fast and pray so that the Lord can heal your tired spirit and build you up to fight the next challenge He has in store for you? The rest and the regimen of fasting, praying, and studying is only worthwhile if you use it to God's will, His glory, and His purpose. I'd hate to think I trained all winter and spring just to continue to train during the season or even worse to quit riding in June. What a waste.

Okay, now I'm ready to put on the cold weather gear, get the old bike out, and brave the 40 degree winter. I can almost smell the spring flowers now....

Chapter 8

SAY IT AIN'T SO

The past few years have been especially bad for the image of cycle racing. A few scandals began to emerge in the late eighties and grew more frequent into the nineties involving cheating, performance enhancing drug usage, secret agreements between riders, and a full selection of other hints of less than honorable competition. A few official efforts were made to curtail a trend toward cheating in the highest ranks of the sport that seemed to be token efforts and hardly impacted the growing problem.

As the scandals persisted, apathy seemed to eclipse objections to curtailing the corruption. Every sort of justification emerged as rational for, sort of, looking the other way. Occasionally a rider or a soigneur would be disciplined for blatant substance abuse violations. On the rare occasion, a coach or team manager would get caught and be given a symbolic chastisement. No one really seemed to be taking the problem seriously. Three-time Tour De France winner Greg Lemond has commented that the peloton seemed to have changed and the doping problem surfaced after his last Tour win in 1990. He questions the performance improvements of some of the riders he competed with during his career. He has been an outspoken and unabashed opponent of doping in the sport.

As the decade of the nineties progressed, so did the use of performance enhancing drugs. Claims flourished that the pressure to win was so demanding and the competition so intense that riders felt the necessity to accept any and every advantage possible. Defenses were (and continue to be) lodged that, "everyone in professional cycling is doing it." "If everyone is doing it, then otherwise clean riders *must* participate in the doping technique just to remain competitive." Many people, both riders and fans, justify cheating by rationalizing that if everyone is cheating, then in all reality it's actually fair. No one has an advantage if all are equally corrupt. Hmmmm. Abandonment of rules levels the playing field. If all are corrupt, none are villains.

At the same time as drug use seemed to be escalating, popularity for cycle racing was too.

SADDLE SORE SPIRITUALITY

Greg Lemond had become the first American to win the coveted Tour De France. He invaded a European dominated sport, won handily, and became an American hero. His popularity, and cycling's, skyrocketed in 1989 when he managed to return to the highest levels of cycling after suffering a near-fatal shotgun wound while bird-hunting in April of 1987. He contested the '89 Tour De France in what may still be the most thrilling Tour in the history of that event and won by a mere eight seconds. After something like 2,300 miles of wheel to wheel battling with some of the greatest athletes ever to put foot to pedal, he won by eight seconds. EIGHT SECONDS! His last-day triumphant time trial around the Champs-Élysées remains as the fastest individual time trial in Tour history, and it was broadcast nationwide, live, during prime Sunday afternoon sports viewing slots. The American people were hooked. We had a genuine comeback kid who won the biggest sporting contest in the world against all odds. He even snatched his victory out of the jaws of defeat with an epic come-from-behind effort on the last lap of the last stage of the greatest race in the world. What a story! Lemond is a genuine likeable guy too. He has that kid-next-door sort of personality. He is a fierce and relentless competitor, but he is also honest, fair and humble.

Millions of Americans were exposed to the great sport of cycling during that period. We, as a nation, knew very little about cycling; but now we had a reason to embrace it, and we were eager to learn. The big Television networks—ESPN, ABC, and little-known OLN—started showing cycling in prime-sports time slots. Cycling savvy sports commentators educated the public about the peculiarities, strategies, demands, and thrill of cycling. Greg Lemond had brought cycling into prominence. Other Americans surfaced as great riders also: Andy Hampstead, George Hincapie, Bob Roll, Davis Phiney, and Frankie Andreau to name a few. Along with the Americans the already famous (in Europe) stars jumped aboard the publicity express train.

Along with the popularity came the money. Big name business and corporate sponsors realized the potential of cycling as an advertising venue. Millions were quickly poured into the business of the sport in North America as well as Europe and Australia. Even though cycling has been important to the rest of the world for decades, the enclaves of cycling recognized the importance and potential of American involvement and its related markets.

Riders were now able to negotiate for real money contracts. Formerly unheard-of million dollar contracts were now being offered to promising stars. Product endorsements and the money associated with them sought successful riders. The winners of the major races were pursued by advertisers and given huge endorsement deals. Champions now are able to divide their prize money among their domestiques who sacrifice so relentlessly to make victory possible for their captain. Many could actually make more money in endorsements than prize money.

Television contracts meant even more money streaming into the sport/business. Television not only meant more money but more exposure for cycling. Professional riders were becoming household names and some gained celebrity status. After Andy Hempstead won the gyro de Italia in 1988 he was greeted by throngs of fans wearing pink shirts when he arrived home at the Denver airport. The Gyro leader's jersey is pink. Hampstead certainly didn't expect anything like that homecoming reception. He relates that during the transatlantic flight someone asked what he had done while in Italy. He had just won the second biggest bike race in the world, but didn't expect Americans to understand that feat much less recognize him. He understatedly told the woman that he had been cycling around Italy with a group of friends. The group of friends was two hundred of the strongest cyclists in the world fighting for the winners pink jersey. The woman was utterly astonished when she emerged from the exit way in the middle of the night into thousands of pink-shirted race fans shouting AN-DEE, AN-DEE!

Through television the average American began to appreciate what cycle racing really is: how demanding it is. I remember in those years when people discovered that I raced bicycles (I love it when people actually think I may be competitive). Uusually they would say something like, "You mean like in the Tour De France?" Occasionally they might say, "...like Greg Lemond?" My head would expand like a balloon and of course I would have to say "yes."

Cycling became mainstream. No one wanted to discourage the massive popularity that it was enjoying. No one wanted to discourage the flow of money. Doping and cheating in sports is, after all, almost a given. Compared to the big league team sports, cycling was squeaky clean. No one was making even much of a perfunctory effort to clean up football or baseball. Those guys were taking things that would make important body parts fall off! The things cyclists were taking were more like over-the-counter pain medications compared to the steroids in most other big-time

SADDLE SORE SPIRITUALITY

sports. And, to be fair, cycling does have probably the most stringent banned substance list in the world. Caffeine is on the list. Yes, something like five cups of joe before a race can get a rider busted. Five cups of Jittery Joe's (now that's some good coffee) can get you busted two weeks later! Aspirin, Tylenol, and most OTC pain medications are banned. Back in '88 or '89 my son broke his foot just before the Tour of The Future. The race doctor could only give him Alka Seltzer for the pain. That wasn't much help! Everything else was on "The List." He rode seven days with a broken foot and no pain reliever and finished, I think, third. Try that in football. The shots that many football players get at halftime just to get them numb enough to get back out on the field would cause abuse-meltdown in cycling. Watch a race on television and notice when an injured rider pulls up to the Race Physician's car the doctor often sprays on a topical medication to cuts and abrasions. That spray is really nothing more than a surface antibiotic that does little more than take the sting out of the boo-boo. Anything more powerful is banned.

Blood is on "the list." Well, let me qualify that. Supercharged, fortified, supplemented, and engineered blood is on "the list." Doctors take blood—either the athlete's or someone else's—and boost the red cell population in it. I don't know how they do that: I think it employs lightning rods and towns folks with pitchforks. That enriched blood is then transfused back into the athlete. The elevated red cell count is able to carry more oxygen to the muscle cells and dramatically improve endurance performance. None-the-less, it's blood.

This spring a newspaper article covered a local pro football player who had gotten into some problems with the authorities. Someone involved with the athlete stated that he had to get cleaned up before spring practice started meaning that he had to stop taking recreational drugs before the team started random testing for the upcoming season. Not so in cycling. Pro cyclists are required to inform their licensing agencies of their whereabouts 365 days a year. They must be eligible for drug testing whenever and wherever the agency chooses. Cyclists must provide an extensive itinerary in advance and inform the agency of any changes to their whereabouts. Failure to be available for one of these out-of-competition tests is considered a violation. Three such violations equal a positive, and the rider is charged and subject to suspension. What other sport requires their athletes to be available out-of-competition and subject to testing at all times?

SADDLE SORE SPIRITUALITY

Don't mistake my overview of "the list" for excusing athletes who abuse it. I'm just putting things in perspective. Undoubtedly the substances included have some ill effect, especially if ingested in large enough quantities or if engineered: like blood doping. Experts don't even know what long-term side effects many of the substances have. But, coffee? Coffee is—well—nutrition. I could probably get bused for caffeine by just going to a race as a spectator. If we are going to have physical, athletic competition; then let it be drug free: all drug free. The human body is a magnificent thing and can produce amazing feats all on its own. Yes, I advocate pure athletics.

The 1998 Tour De France—Cycling's premier race—was dubbed the Tour De Dopage (say that with a phony French, nasal accent) when Team Festina and its elite riders were discharged from the race after police found large quantities of doping products in the possession of the team soigneur. Authorities then conducted a series of midnight raids at the hotel rooms of Festina and several other teams participating in the race. Imagine racing 120 miles, day after day, and then being rousted by a police goon-squad in the middle of the night so they could check your shaving kit for needles. One may be a little cranky at the breakfast table. The race was in jeopardy as several of the teams withdrew and sent their riders home not wishing to be treated in such a gorilla-like fashion. At one point, the entire peloton staged a sit-down protest to demonstrate its disgust at the handling of the whole incident. The future of the then nearly one hundred year old Tour De France was threatened as well as perhaps professional cycling itself.

The Tour survived, and cycling survived. Many close to the sport speculated that it had cleaned out the "dirty" riders and re-leveled the playing field as much as a cycle race in two of the world's most challenging mountain ranges can be termed "level." The governing bodies, the teams and the sponsors pledged to keep the sport clean.

Well, that didn't work for long. The following year, 1999, brought Lance Armstrong to the center podium with his first of seven consecutive wins. During his reign, cheating and doping allegations plagued the American champion constantly. Even after his retirement in 2005 the accusations continued. Armstrong has never wavered in his denial of cheating; claiming to have been the most dope-tested cyclist in history but never having posted a positive result. Now there's a story to tell your grandchildren sitting on your knee. "Ya know kids; Gramps got to tee-tee in a plastic cup more than anyone else in history."

SADDLE SORE SPIRITUALITY

Over the past ten years or so, cycling has indeed discovered and disciplined a multitude of dopers and cheaters. Some of the great names of the recent modern era have been found to be "dirty." And, when each one was discovered we wishful fans would sort of collectively cringe with embarrassment, the press would predict the demise of cycling as if it were the fall of democracy, and we would all hope that this would finally clean up the sport once and for all. I'd hate to guess how many times I have said that "This will be the year of clean, rider-against-rider racing. No one would dare take the chance of getting busted now." Then, one by one, the icons fell.

As the testing technology became more sophisticated and the ruling bodies became more determined to enforce its power, so did cheating technology. Insiders said that the science of testing for illegal substances was just a half step behind the science of producing illegal substances: something like the traffic cop having the second fastest car in town.

After Armstrong retired, most experts agreed that the sport was clean and that the scandals were over. OOPS! Just a few hours before the 2006 Tour De France, Operation Puerto broke loose. Spanish authorities publically released their long-term investigation into Doctor Eufemiano

Fuentes and his alleged practice of supplying illegal substances to perhaps hundreds of world-class athletes including many of cycling's top names. Most of the riders who were thought to be contenders to reign after Lance Armstrong were banned from riding the Tour De France that year. Some were later cleared of any wrongdoing. Some have never recovered and either been judged with lengthy suspensions or have retired in shame.

Finally, a clean race! Who could be so bold—so stupid—as to try to race "dirty" after all this? 2006 would be a great year for cycling. Finally we could see pure, unaided rider against rider: challenges overcome by pure human, physical ability and skill.

As it turned out, the 2006 race was a thriller from prologue to the final lap around the Champs-Élysées. To the dismay of many Frenchmen, American Floyd Landis won in a breathtaking finish. "La Americans ween our la race ageeen. Eeat is eight times. Is not goooood for France!"

Landis is a likeable sort of guy brought up as a Mennonite in the farm country of Pennsylvania. He was racing with a degenerated right hip that would stop most people from walking to the refrigerator. He, however, rode the toughest mountains in the world through all that pain. He seemed to be the All-American-Hero.

SADDLE SORE SPIRITUALITY

Landis was winning and wearing the Yellow Jersey and all but sure to win it all at the beginning of mountain Stage 16: the second to the last mountain stage in the '06 tour. Now, everyone has a bad day once in a while. I personally have been known to have a bad day three or four times a week. It just happens with no warning and no logical explanation. The legs just refuse to go. If it happens during a ride it's called the "BONK." If it happens from the very start of the ride, it's just a bad day. No matter how willing the brain is to power on through, the legs feel like logs: they are heavy, painful, slow, and weak. The lungs refuse to process enough oxygen to fuel the body. Every fiber of every cell of every muscle hurts. It is the most debilitating feeling anyone can experience on a bike. Nothing helps. It only gets worse. Well, Floyd had his bad day to beat all bad days on Stage 16. That's not a good time for the mule to balk. He lost something over ten minutes on that one stage. He went from first to eleventh place eight minutes eight seconds behind in the overall standings. The Yellow Jersey was gone and without a miracle the race was lost. What he had spent his whole life trying to accomplish was gone in one four-hour stage. He was devastated. He had not only disappointed himself, but he felt he had let his team mates down: those guys who had sacrificed everything, everyday of the Tour for him. I know even I felt demoralized. I thought the nice, clean-cut guy from a good Christian home would bring victory to America yet again. Now it seemed all was lost.

Landis suffered his humiliation that night, but refused to give up. In his humiliation he devised a plan. He had given opportunity to the other contenders that day and they attacked with vengeance. His rivals tried to take full advantage of his weak moment. With Floyd out, they fought each other to near collapse for the coveted *Maillot Jaune:* the Yellow Jersey. So, that meant that they would all be exhausted from fighting each other for the lead and be willing to rest tomorrow. I know, "rest" is a bizarre word to use for cyclists in a stage race. And, as much time as he had lost, no one would imagine he could ever make it up. His plan: he would attack at the bottom of the very first climb of the day. He would need the entire day's ride to have any chance of gaining enough time to be a threat again. No serious contender attacks that early. They would not chase him: after all, attacks that early in a stage rarely succeed. What did he have to lose?

Well, one strange phenomenon about bonking and bad days is that, usually, the next day is great. I guess the body figurers that it's better to make up for being bad by being especially good the next day. Children have that same sort of logic.

His team mates gave their blessing more out of respect than accord. Rumor of his plan soon spread throughout the peloton the morning of stage 17, but most did not believe he would try or could succeed even if he did. He let his team lead him as much as they could until they dropped back one by one from fatigue. By the end of the first climb, Floyd was alone and in the lead. As he had predicted, no one was willing to chase. No one thought he could possibly have enough strength to stay out front for the entire stage. And, just like he had strategized, the main challengers were too weak from yesterday's ride to mount much of a counter-attack.

He rode like a man possessed. Some four hours later he raised a jubilant, almost angry fist in the air as he crossed the finish line alone and first: minutes ahead of anyone else. He had given himself the possibility to win. In fact two days later he gained enough time in the individual time trial to regain the Yellow Jersey and the race. He won the Tour De France. The all American boy had given us the perfect Tour.

The celebration for us and for Floyd was short lived. Only a day or two (just hours) after his magnificent comeback victory, rumors started emerging that one of the riders—a big name—had tested positive for a banned substance. It was Floyd Landis. He had failed the Stage winner's mandatory drug screening after his epic victory of stage 17. Proponents of strict doping control had finally proclaimed that they had proven that cheating was rampant at the highest level of cycling and that they would not allow even a popular champion to escape. Fans were demoralized. His dream for victory and our dream for a clean peloton had forever vanished. He continues to declare his innocence as he has done since he was first accused. He has fought and appealed every accusation, decision, and chastisement relating to the charges. The case is still not determined more than a year later.

So, 2007 surely would be a clean, dope-free, controversy-free season. The powers-that-be must certainly have frightened any rider from even thinking about employing a banned substance or cheating in any way. The peloton loved it: they could compete based on physical ability, strategy, and skill. The press was impressed. The fans were energized. Without the "supercharged" athletes the racing was more exciting than ever. Clean is good!Oops again. The 2007 Giro d'Italia—The Tour of Italy: the second most prestigious race

SADDLE SORE SPIRITUALITY

of the season—was marred by controversy which was later determined to be false. The winner was barred from competing in the Tour De France while his case was being heard. Okay, nothing like a little scare to keep honest people honest.

In the early stages of the 2007 Tour De France no one could predict who might emerge as an ultimate overall race leader. The racing was thrilling and thought to be at long last, clean. Only over a week into the three week campaign the doping allegations started again. By the end of the race four riders had tested positive for banned substances: among them were two of the pre-race favorites. The man who emerged in the last half as the race leader and all but certain winner was sent home by his own team for violating team and UCI (Union Cycliste Internationale: International Cycling Union) rules. His own team felt he had been at least dishonest. The eventual winner has a cloud of controversy hanging over him stemming from the Operation Puerto investigation of which he was cleared. Doubt still lingers in press innuendo.

So the sport took another devastating hit. Will this last bombardment finally drive the cheaters either out of cycling or away from dishonesty? Or, will it completely destroy the sport? Several of the major teams have disbanded either out of disgrace or lack of sponsorship. Certainly the highest levels of professional cycling have suffered (to use a boxing cliché) a knockdown. Cycling is expensive and corporate money is essential. Some say the pressure from sponsors is what is causing riders to seek chemical, performance-enhancing supplements. I say cheaters are cheaters: the money only exposes the character of those who are willing.

Riders are not the only villains in this soap opera. Team directors, coaches, and doctors have been found to be complicit in cheating. Even some of the governing associations themselves have been suspected of contributing to the problem. Scotsman Graeme Obree, two time World Hour Record holder and two time Individual Pursuit World Champion, alludes to pressure that took him out of road racing. He implies that after he was selected by a major European road race team he was pressured to use the team doctor and to take certain "vitamins and supplements." He refused on both issues and was dismissed from the team. Anonymous reports of that same sort of pressure are rampant, but most aspiring riders don't resist the pressure. To make matters worse, the peloton seems to have some code of silence, and rarely does anyone come forth with first-hand information. See no evil, hear no evil, and certainly speak no evil.

SADDLE SORE SPIRITUALITY

Doubt exists that most of the governing bodies are of any help at all and may perhaps even be part of the problem. International racing and Riders are governed under the UCI as well as their own national cycling organizations. USA Cycling is the American association that governs and licenses professional cyclists for the United States. Rules seem to be pinned for the benefit of the associations and leave riders vulnerable to the power of the overbearing bureaus. Riders have no say-so and rules exist—and are enforced—prohibiting riders from criticizing policies, rules, or decisions: so much for the First Amendment. If riders stray too far from the edicts of the powerful national/international organizations they are severely dealt with and perhaps ostracized. Careers can be ended. Riders learn quickly to fall into and stay in line.

If a rider is accused of breaking one of the many rules, he is suspended pending a hearing. Does that sound like punishment before being proven guilty? The hearing is carried out by the national association of which the rider is licensed. If found guilty, the rider may appeal, but the appeal is waged to and through the association that levied the verdict in the first place. The rider may request arbitration to settle a case. Guess what? The panel of arbiters is selected by the—you got it—association that levied the charges to begin with. And to add more power to the court, the association gets to determine what evidence may be presented and who may testify. Oh yes, the accusing association may restrict discovery: the defendant's right to know what evidence is being presented against him. Kangaroo Court?

Not only is the list of banned substances all-inclusive, the labs that test these athletes are less than perfect. In fact the standards vary from nation to nation and from lab to lab. A positive test in France may be declared perfectly legal in Australia for instance. Labs are rarely held accountable to maintain the standards set forth by the client anti-doping agencies. In two well publicized cases labs continued to process samples that were mislabeled. Strict chain of custody was neglected. Lab technicians had knowledge of whose samples they were testing and confidentiality was ignored. Athletes were, regardless, convicted and careers severely damaged.

Cycling has no riders union like football or most of the other big league team sports. Teams are in the business of winning races, therefore they have very little time or money to defend individual riders. Sponsors are in this for advertising and stay as far from controversial publicity as possible. So, if accused, guilty or not; riders are on their own. Most riders don't have the money to fight their defense. Many proclaim innocence but suffer suspensions because they simply can't afford to defend themselves.

Some have said that the sport will not survive: that the public and potential sponsors will no longer associate with such a dirty business. Others say that this may be its best hour: showing the rest of the sports world that perseverance can purify any meaningful endeavor. Whoever ends up being correct, the scandal is devastating, demoralizing, and embarrassing. If cycling, which has the most stringent and comprehensive banned substance list and enforcement policy in sports, can survive; all the other sports can pay attention, take notes, and follow suit.

Will professional cycle racing survive? Probably. I have no doubt that it will change forever. It may never be as big as it once was or could have been. The epic tours may be in big trouble. Money drives all professional sports and corporate advertisers are running from cycling like cats from rocking chairs. They may come back, but slowly and carefully.

Will cycling survive? Without a doubt! You see, the millions of average riders like you and me pedaling for health, enjoyment, and personal pleasure will not be dissuaded by the detrimental actions of a few elite racers. Whatever scandal occurs cannot change what cycling does for each one of us out on the road every day. We will still get the same benefit from that afternoon ride whether a million dollar professional rider is clean or dirty. It won't change what the bike does for the rest of us. Why? Because we love what we do, and our sport loves us back. We simply are not affected in our day-to-day cycling lives by misconduct at the top. We love our bikes and our bikes have not changed. Cycling is still going to give us the same health benefits that it always has. It will still give us the freedom that drew us to it in the first place. It will still be a glorious stress reliever. It will still make us feel good after a ride. Our pleasure and benefit from the bicycle does not depend on the purity of those few who choose to defile the sport.

Some of the great races may suffer. Team budgets and riders' salaries may suffer. We may see less cycling on television. Perhaps that isn't a bad thing. Instead of watching cycling we may have more time and initiative to get off the couch and go out and ride. The only drawback is that the message that cycling is good for everyone may not get exposure. What a shame that might be for our youth who may never be enticed to try the wonder of cycling.

SADDLE SORE SPIRITUALITY

Local cycling clubs will survive and most likely even thrive. They will because as much as we like to ride alone we like to join in company with others that feel the same way. Large amounts of corporate advertising dollars are not involved. Large amounts of camaraderie are. A million dollar purse may not be waiting for any of us at the finish of a Saturday morning club ride, but the competition is just as fierce and the pride just as great when we are the first to crest *"the big hill"* or when we win the sprint for the city limit sign. A million dollars: no. A million dollars worth of pride and accomplishment: absolutely! We have and will retain our local Tours de Fun. The bike hasn't changed nor has its rewards.

So where are we today? 1. We have scandals at the highest levels of the sport involving the participants as well as those who are supposed to be in charge of leading them and the sport itself. 2. Riders at all levels are not abiding by the rules. 3. Money is bearing pressure on leaders throughout the sport to do whatever it takes to promote their agenda and gain power. 4. Governing bodies are trying to save themselves at the expense of struggling participants. 5. The entire institution of the sport at its peak level is perhaps in jeopardy. 6. Promising athletes are avoiding cycling because of the negative image it is exposed to. 7. Youth, up and coming riders, are not being exposed the benefits of cycling. What a shame for them.

The past few years have been especially bad for the image of religion. Scandals began to emerge in the late seventies and early eighties involving some of the very large and influential ministries throughout the world. In the beginning the stories seemed to be associated mostly with the new evangelical and primarily independent movements. They were, or at least they seemed to be, the fringe of the religious world. As time went on we have been somewhat enlightened to the depth of corruption in the church. The indiscretions of the "fringe" have led to uncovering the improprieties of mainstream denominations. In many ways this disrepute associated with organized religion—the church—parallels that of cycling in the time frame that it became public and many of the tactics used to confront it. In many respects the base causes are quite similar. The results, however, are tragically different.

To a certain extent, the demise of some of the giant televangelist and evangelical ministries of the seventies, eighties and onward were predictable and could have been expected. Their rapid and uncontrolled growth in following and in wealth seemed like a recipe for corruption. To a cynical, not-very-religious world these ministries had the appearance of a readymade con game. To spiritually starved followers they provided daily inspiration, hope, and teaching that were not being provided by mainstream denominations or local, traditional churches. They were in fact filling a spiritual void. Christians tired of the lifeless, ho-hum, always-the-same service at local church were exposed to new and exciting worship. People were introduced to a joy of worship. The great old hymns gave way to lively new music. Sermons avoided "Thou Shall NOT!" and embraced "You are capable of anything through Christ!"

Earnest, Godly ministers could barely keep pace with the world's thirst for live and personal spirituality. Congregations grew exponentially, and budgets demanded proportional growth. Holy men and women of God who had spent their lives struggling suddenly found themselves in charge of massive ministries and corporation-like financing. Some gained national and worldwide fame: even celebrity status. The spiral seemed to be limitless. Not unlike kings and leaders of the Old Testament, fortune and success begat corruption, greed, and mismanagement.

I have no doubt that the overwhelming majority of ministry leaders who fall from grace are convinced in their own spirit that they are doing good. Oh yes I also know that churches and religious movements are ripe for ethical degenerates and straight-out con artists. I've met several of them. I've fallen victim to one or two of them.

During that period of rapid growth in the religious world all sorts of made-for-the-movies scenarios unfolded in real life. We had the extravagances of the evangelical organizations. Some became so wealthy that they claimed the extravagances were rewards from God and were manifestations of the love of God for His faithful children. Now I am sure that God wants for his children to have life and have it more abundantly, but gold plated faucets and air conditioned dog houses may have gone just a little too far. I don't believe that ministers must live a life of poverty to do God's work, but these are not the only two options. Maybe ceiling fans for the dog house might have been a bit more in keeping.

We were awakened too to the carnal improprieties (ah-hum) of some of the great preachers of the flat screen. While preaching with great animation, conviction, and a southern accent against the sins of the flesh some of the so-called leaders of the new religious movement were busy doing sermon research of the personal kind in all sorts of interesting places with all sorts of interesting people: ah, research assistants. Now I am not too naïve as to think this sort of hanky-panky had not gone on throughout history, but rarely had it been publicized so openly nor involved such highly esteemed figures.

Greed crept into the movement as well. Oh, what a surprise! Millions upon millions of dollars were being poured into these ministries at warp speed. Much of the money went to honest and honorable causes. Much of it went to gold faucets and air conditioned dog houses. Ministries seemed to have the overwhelming need to grow larger and larger sort of like government agencies. The funds needed just to administratively sustain these now-international organizations is enormous. They became their own television networks. They opened national and international offices. They diversified their holdings just like Fortune 500 corporations do. Ministries invested—for the KINGdommm-ah—in hotels, resorts, theme parks, universities, investment companies, and real estate. Many were, and remain, legitimate and mission-based. Many were scams. Many fell someplace in between. They were all concerned about money. The sudden influx of huge sums of money brought pressure on the organizations to grow, and the growth demanded more and more money. That sort of stress will cause righteous men into unrighteous behavior. It will entice unrighteous men to its bounty.

Religion became mainstream. We could watch any number of inspiring programs anytime day or night. Pick your preacher by style, costume, hairdo or size of church. We could go to colossal crusades that filled football stadiums. We could even take a vacation at a biblical resort complex complete with in-room prayer closet and unlimited foot-washings.

Was any of this inherently bad? I actually think it simply got out of hand. Ministers with good hearts and good intentions got swallowed up in the explosive growth of it all. Most were ill-prepared to control the massive amounts of money and fame that flash-flooded them. Remember, for decades previous most religious movements were struggling just to exist. Was any of this good? Oh, I certainly believe so. In spite of the problems that crept into the heart of the movement, poor were fed, sick were healed, abandoned souls were rescued, lonely were befriended, lost were found. These religious kingdoms were founded for the most part on honorable motives.

We were involved in one church that had miraculously grown from a small congregation to a large and prosperous body under the guidance of a dynamic and flamboyant young minister. He was a cross between Billy Sunday and Elvis in a bright yellow suit. Souls were being saved. The sick were being healed. The body was experiencing true and meaningful worship that it had never imagined before. Margaret and I (Margaret more so than I) observed that when the man preached it was as if God had been speaking to us the second time with the same heavenly message. Perhaps the preacher was only confirming what the Lord was telling us personally. It was not until after his fall from grace did we come to know the real man in the canary costume.

Our young son wakened us early one Saturday with the morning newspaper asking what was Brother Bubba (that's not his real name of course) doing in handcuffs on the front page? Now that will make for an interesting breakfast-table discussion. So it turned out, Brother Bubba was certainly not what he seemed to be. He ended up on the front page after being arrested by federal agents for running drugs from South America along with several other charges.

Further investigation unveiled that he was sort of the Swiss Army Knife of the downfallen clergy set. Name it and he was into it. Among some of his more dreadful behavior some of the staff discovered that he had been recording the sermons of a well known television minister and (with the help of a lovely, young assistant) transcribing them for presentation as his own the following week or so. We were hearing the exact sermon that we had heard on television but coming out of the mouth of our Brother Bubba with a very flamboyant presentation. Oh, he was good at it too. Actually, he had a better presentation than the original preacher: more animated.

Tragically, in recent months, we are hearing revolting stories of unthinkable sins deep in the bowels of well established religions. Many of these sins have scarred young victims intensely and for life. We are finding that these transgressions have been deeply embedded in reputable religions for decades. More tragically however is the fact that some religious stalwarts knew of the behavior of church officials, did nothing about it, and then hid it as long as possible. Now, even after the light of public scrutiny has been shown upon the transgressions, the well-established religious institutions are cleansing their sin by out-of-court settlements with the exact sums of the payoffs not disclosed. Sad.

Oh the shame is not limited to the mega-ministries. Local, independent churches are having their own scandals. The First Piety Church on the corner of Main Street and Pearl Gate Avenue may be an architectural tribute to purity on the outside, but has harbored dark activities within its halls for decades. As a youngster I can remember overhearing my parent's conversations with other church members discussing the rapid dismissal of more than one pastor or deacon. I didn't catch all of the hushed discussions nor did I decipher what they were talking about for years to come, but putting two and two together I have no doubt that some of these church leaders were not without sin: deep sin.

We were involved in another church—not the Elvis preacher church—that had its problems. It was rocked by the arrest of its assistant pastor for soliciting a male prostitute. That was tough enough until one Sunday morning a few months later a lady stood after altar call and asked if she could speak. She proceeded to confess—scripturally—that she had been having an affair with the pastor. Oh how awful! Well awful was surpassed when three other ladies stood and asked, "You Too?"

So, you see, sin in the ministry is not limited to large and money-corrupted mega-churches. Hypocrisy infiltrates all levels and all aspects of organized religion from the pew to the board room. Are all professing Christians corrupt? No. Are all religious organizations corrupt? No. Just like cycling, a few overzealous individuals are degrading the image of the entire movement. Sad.

Will the church survive? It will. God has

ordained it. *"...upon this rock I will build my church; **and the gates of hell shall not prevail against it.**"* Matthew 16:18. I have no doubt that it will change. It already has. Most of the gaudy mega-ministries have crumbled. Most of the honorable ones have survived. My personal conviction is that the church—the organized congregations—are in decline because they are in the entertainment business having lost sight of the awesome commission of shepherding the flock. Their main function today is to grow by numbers and programs, not by souls served for the King. I know many saints of God who no longer attend services because they are sick of the entertainment and the circus that is prevalent in local churches today. They—churches—are offering deliverance from the "world" by becoming like the "world." People are seeking spirituality, going to church to find it, and being given the world they are trying to overcome. They already have the emptiness of that. It will stop! God is waiting for a bride, a church, without blemish.

*"⁷Let us be glad and rejoice, and give honour to him: for the marriage of the Lamb is come, and his wife hath made herself ready. ⁸And to her was granted that she **should be arrayed in fine linen, clean and white:***

for the fine linen is the righteousness of saints. *⁹And he saith unto me, Write, Blessed are they which are called unto the marriage supper of the Lamb. And he saith unto me, These are the true sayings of God."*
Revelation 19:7-9

"²⁵Husbands, love your wives, even as Christ also loved the church, and gave himself for it; ²⁶That he might sanctify and cleanse it with the washing of water by the word, ²⁷That he might present it to himself ***a glorious church, not having spot, or wrinkle, or any such thing; but that it should be holy and without blemish."***
Ephesians 5:25 - 27

Will Christianity survive? It will, and it will grow and purify itself. You see, when Jesus died on the cross and overcame death and the grave HE became our source: not the priest, not the pastor, not the deacon, not the church. The power of the one and only GOD is as real and as individual as ever. Our faith does not depend on the brick and mortar church, but on Christ Himself.

The peace, blessings, and daily joy we have in Christ shall never fade because HE is our source. HIS blessings are individual to each one of us. You see, the millions of average Christians like you and me believing on His promises for health, enjoyment, and personal faith will not be dissuaded by the detrimental actions of a few misguided ministers. We will still get that same benefit from prayer and true worship of HIM whether a few elite ministers are clean or dirty. Our spiritual connection is directly to the King. It is personal. His faithfulness will always endure. We love our LORD and that will never change! HE loves us and that will never change! *"¹⁰For the mountains shall depart, and the hills be removed; but my kindness shall not depart from thee, neither shall the covenant of my peace be removed, saith the LORD that hath mercy on thee. ¹¹O thou afflicted, tossed with tempest, and not comforted, behold, I will lay thy stones with fair colours, and lay thy foundations with sapphires.* Isaiah 54:10-11 Our pleasure and joy from the Lord does not depend on the purity of those few who choose to defile the church.

HIS word is true and endures forever. Remember the Elvis Church? As seemingly corrupt as that pastor was, people were still saved and healed and blessed by the sermons that he preached. HIS word, GOD'S Word, is true no matter who utters it. *"¹⁰For as the rain cometh down, and the snow from heaven, and returneth not thither, but watereth the earth, and maketh it bring forth and bud, that it may give seed to the sower, and bread to the eater:* **¹¹So shall my word be that goeth forth out of my mouth: it shall not return unto me void, but it shall accomplish that which I please, and it shall prosper in the thing whereto I sent it.** *¹²For ye shall go out with joy, and be led forth with peace: the mountains and the hills shall break forth before you into singing, and all the trees of the field shall clap their hands.* Isaiah 55:10 -12. You see, Pastor Bubba was repeating the sermons of a righteous minister, and that minister was using the inspired Word of God. Pastor Bubba was unknowingly preaching the words of GOD. The message was pure no matter how corrupt the messenger. Its power is absolute!

So where are we today? 1. We have scandals throughout the organized church involving the congregation as well as those who are supposed to be the priests—the ministers—leading the faithful. 2. Christians at all levels are not abiding by the Word. 3. Money is bearing pressure on leaders throughout the church to do whatever it takes to promote their ministry and gain power. 4. Church leaders are trying to save themselves at the expense of the flock. 5. The entire organized church is perhaps in jeopardy. 6. Good and Godly people are avoiding organized religions because of the negative image it is exposing. 7. Youth, up and coming saints, are not being exposed to the blessings of God. What a shame for them.

"33But seek ye first the kingdom of God, and his righteousness; and all these things shall be added unto you. 34Take therefore no thought for the morrow: for the morrow shall take thought for the things of itself. Sufficient unto the day is the evil thereof."
Matthew 6:33 - 34

Just like you continue to enjoy the bike for its inherent virtues, never stop seeking God and all his glory for the only true peace and happiness you will find. He will never fail you.

Chapter 9

PROPER ETIQUETTE PLEASE

I've made a few attempts at playing golf: feeble attempts. They were all unqualified disasters! Still, every few years I sort of get the bug to try it again until I remember how demoralized I felt after those early struggles. Now, I had some great teachers along the way too. My lovely wife's uncles made some valiant endeavors to mentor me and actually never gave up despite my, what must have looked like slapstick comedy, studentship. My wife is from Scotland. Her whole family are accomplished golfers. They grew up on the courses of West Scotland and are all very good. They're Scots; what did I expect? They were so good that they knew exactly how to play the tides and waves on the course next to the Ocean. Really! I was once told to hit a tee shot out over the ocean ninety degrees to the green. Ohhhh-kay? But, being instructed to wait until the wave came in was a little too much for my logic process. "NOW, HIT IT NOW!" I was shouted to with a distinct Scottish accent. It worked. The ball sailed in the wrong direction, did a perfect loop curve way out over the cliffs, lifted, and hooked back perfectly onto the green. The trick I'm told was to hit it to coincide with an incoming wave of adequate size. It has something to do with the ocean winds and the air turbulence from the wave giving lift to the ball, and.... Now that's good! They were such good teachers that I gave up out of humiliation—and relative lack of talent.

Golf looks like a great sport though: a casual walk around some beautiful landscape in the fresh air. As I get older, my temperament may have mellowed enough for me to accept my mediocre performance. Maybe. One thing I really respect about the game is the etiquette honored by the players. Golfers respect one another. They respect the game. As frustrating as the game may be, they adhere to a time honored code of behavior. I like the way they allow others to play through rather than hold up someone else. They keep quiet while others putt. They put divots back in place. I recently read an article about a pro golfer who called a foul on himself for inadvertently using two different balls on the same hole. Who knew that was illegal? He alerted the official knowing that it would cost him a severe penalty. In fact, it cost him the match and in turn cost him a spot on the pro tour. Now that's respecting the game. He was okay with that. I'd sort of be concerned about my own honesty in that situation.

Golf and golfers, I'm certain, are as athletic, skilled, and competitive as cyclists. I've photographed golf tournaments, and that leisurely walk around the course can become as severe as waging war on a rolling-hill battlefield: traps, trenches and all. Golfers may be nice to one another, but they are savage competitors through the eighteenth hole. And, as far as the game is concerned they take no prisoners. It's a physically tough game too! I only photograph an event and I take three days to recover.

Many other sports are the same. Tennis has its etiquette. I'm not sure what that is, but I know it exists. Cursing the line official probably isn't one of the articles in their code of behavior. Even football, as brutal as that game is, has etiquette. They introduce themselves to one another, shake hands and—after bashing the other guy to a bloody, muddy pulp—hug and congratulate the beast who just broke your team's nose.

Cycling has its conventions and decorum too,

PROPER ETIQUETTE PLEASE

believe it or not! Logic may suggest that simply riding around the neighborhood with a few friends shouldn't require anything more than common, everyday social skills. Now think about it: even a casual, friendly ride around the neighborhood with a buddy turns into an unannounced competition. No one wants to show weakness. Monday rides—rest day rides—always start off with someone saying, "Let's take it easy today: how about we have a really easy ride. No one push today, Okay?" "OKAY!" Everybody agrees. After all, we all just had a hard weekend on the bike either racing or touring up the biggest mountain in the state. Right? We all need a really nice, easy ride. By the end of this leisurely trek the whole group is attacking like a pack of hounds about to catch the fox.

And, it always starts off that way: "Let's just have an easy ride today." But, sometime during the ride the law of half-wheeling comes into effect. Half-wheeling as I discussed in Chapter six is a cycling phenomenon that cannot be controlled. It's a law of nature. Once it starts, it has a life of its own. It starts off innocently enough with two riders going at an easy, comfortable pace. They are probably having a pleasant conversation about the Book of Luke, enjoying the scenery, and glad for the chance to ride slowly. Then it happens. And on it goes until these two are down on the drops at full speed and gasping for air. When they collapse at the end of the ride, someone always says, "I thought we were going to have an easy ride!"

The same scenario happens with a group ride. The only difference is that the rider who takes the pull—the lead rider pushing through the greatest air resistance—thinks he's being weak if he slows the pace. So, he ups the pace just a little on his pull to show that he is not a slacker. The next guy to take the pull has to.... Well you get the idea. The casual, conversational Monday rest ride ends up with a lung busting pack sprint at the city limit sign.

I actually don't know what this all has to do with etiquette, but it does seem to be a very important tradition of the sport: agreeing to an easy ride and cleverly pounding the stuffing out of your best riding partner.

Now don't let me misrepresent the sport. Racing cyclists can be as brutal as professional wrestlers when they need to be. I have been told that out of sight of officials racers have been known to engage in some less than gentlemanly tactics like elbowing the competition, running the other guy off the road, and cleverly pinching someone's rear brake calipers while on a tough climb. I couldn't attest to this myself. These are just stories I have

PROPER ETIQUETTE PLEASE

been told. You didn't see anything, and you can't prove I did it.

However, as naturally competitive as cycling is either as recreational exercise or competitive sport, it has a wonderful set of unwritten and often unstated ethics and protocol. Congress could learn a great deal from the peloton. I think all elected officials should be required by the Constitution to participate in a group ride twice a week.

These rules—guidelines, social suggestions—like I said earlier are not written down anywhere. We don't have an Official Cyclist's Be Nice Handbook. So, the rules of the road are passed down from rider to rider or perhaps more often just by osmosis: ride and observe. As in most social situations, we have a certain percentage who didn't get the memo. Okay, we have a small percentage who got the memo and choose to ignore it. I think some people come into the sport with the mindset of survival of the fittest. The "I'll look good by making you look bad" approach is unacceptable in cycling, but it does exist to a certain extent. I think maybe professional wrestlers converting to cycling is the main contributing faction.

I'll make an attempt to cover some of the more basic guidelines for you. This is not intended to be an exhaustive list. These are just some of the more important guidelines I have learned through the years. These few examples may influence your mindset in relation to cycling decorum.

This first one, I think, is possibly particular to me. Some of my regular riding friends have taken it up and I appreciate that, but not many others have. I would like to see this catch on with everyone. I learned this while riding mountains in France and Italy. On the mountain passes, cars often have no safe opportunity to overtake a cyclist on those long, narrow passes. Not to worry: the drivers would patiently wait behind until it was safe to go around. Then, with the slightest chirp of the horn, on they would go: no impatient ocean liner-like blasting of the horn, no cursing, no attempt to run me off the road, no gunfire. Whenever that happened I would give the driver a friendly wave of the hand and a "thank you" and they would always return the sentiment. I continued this when I began riding daily in Northwest Florida. I wouldn't want to say that the motorists were overly aggressive or anything, but encountering a polite driver was a noteworthy event. So, I thought the well-mannered thing to do was to acknowledge courteous behavior. I started giving a friendly, thank-you wave of the hand to any driver who was considerate to me or to any driver who I may have inconvenienced. Some drivers did not realize that they were being courteous, so the

PROPER ETIQUETTE PLEASE

return sentiment occasionally was a gesture of a different sort.

When I first came to Tennessee I was riding out in Wilson County and struggling half way up one of these monster Tennessee hills when I began to hear the annoyed rattle of a big diesel engine behind me. Uh Oh! It was a narrow road and my climbing legs were not accustomed to—well—climbing. I had no place to pull over. If I slowed any at all I would have toppled over and been immediate road kill. My only option was to continue at a quivering snail's pace and act macho like I was King of the Mountain. The truck crept and rattled along behind. Truck drivers really don't like to creep up hills. As I started to ease onto the crest of the hill, shaking from exhaustion, I managed to glance back and try to look the enemy in the eye. All I could see was the biggest truck's grill I have ever seen. This monster dump truck blocked out the sun! All I could see was red fenders, a dirty chrome grill, and the Peterbilt's red oval logo that looked to me like the front site on an army tank's gun. I knew for certain that this driver was not happy with me. As we both crested the hill the truck eased up beside me while I kept my focus on the road. Out of both courtesy and extreme fear I managed to take my left hand off the bar and give my signature thank you wave.

SADDLE SORE SPIRITUALITY

I was hoping that the truck would just speed on past me, but it only pulled up even with me so that the passenger side door was even with the imaginary target on my back. From my experience in Florida, I assumed the Driver was either reloading or taking careful aim. Since he was not going on past, I nervously and boldly looked up—high up—into the passenger side window of the cab. To my utter amazement the driver had leaned across the cab far enough to be seen, and as soon as I made eye contact he waved a thank-you back to me. I was amazed! The big red dump truck went on down the road and all I could think was "I've found home!" Middle Tennessee continues from that day to produce the most courteous drivers I have encountered in the States. They rank among the best I have seen in the world.

I continue to thank drivers whom I delay and who show courtesy to me. I strongly believe that this slight gesture of appreciation is respected and is contagious. So, try and make a friendly thank-you part of your riding etiquette. Maybe the thought will be paid back to you one day. Maybe drivers will have a better opinion of all cyclists.

Another constant consideration almost all riders practice is calling out warnings while on the road. "Car Back/car up" alerts riders that a car is approaching. "Car left/right" tells others that a

PROPER ETIQUETTE PLEASE

car is at or near an intersecting street. "On your left/right" informs riders that you are overtaking or alongside and from which side. That's really important for everyone. Always keep other riders aware of your position when you are not obviously in their view. I always appreciate the lead rider hollering back "BUMP" for the obvious. Most riders practice pointing to upcoming obstructions, debris, and potholes in the road. "DOG RIGHT" has saved many trips to the emergency room as well as contentious lawsuits. So, make it a practice to keep your fellow riders informed.

Occasionally, just like the cowboy's trusty steed, a bike will throw a shoe out on the trail. Rule #1 is to always carry at least a patch kit and a pump. I like to carry two spare tubes and change the tube instead of trying to patch a hole on the side of the road. Once I had five flats on a single ride. I flatted first at the end of the driveway: should have known it would be a bad day. By flat number five I had used both my spare tubes and all my patches. Walking to the 7-Eleven in cycling cleats is not easy and is extremely humiliating. Calling for someone to come and rescue me is even more difficult. Rule #1a is: replace worn tires before you end up with five flats and out in a lonely country road. Bike tires are very thin to start with, so when they are worn down to the threads almost

SADDLE SORE SPIRITUALITY

anything will cause a puncture. I once flatted from a staple: a common office paper staple. Remember Chapter Two when I said I am very careful with expenses? I do like to get my money's worth out of a set of tires and I occasionally pay the price in flats.

That brings me to the point. Bet you thought I'd never get here didn't you? At some point in your cycling life you will be out on a group ride and someone else will have a problem—a mechanical—and will have forgotten to bring anything to fix it with. The proper thing to do is to give him yours. WHAT, NO "I'LL SELL YOU A TUBE." NO I.O.U? And, don't expect a replacement. Riders share tubes and patches and pumps all the time. I've given away tubes, patches, gloves, sweatbands, money, water bottles, and even Snickers. Believe me, you will be the recipient of something one day. Just think when you donate a tube to an in-need rider it's like depositing one in the First National Cycling Bank Special Tube account. You are likely to need an emergency withdrawal one day. Patches, extra water, Snickers, spare gloves, and what-have-you all fall into that same category.

Along the same line when someone has any problem, stop and help. We don't have the cycle equivalent of AAA. Usually the guy can fix his own flat, but be polite and stop to offer help. More than

PROPER ETIQUETTE PLEASE

once I have seen riders fix a flat only to discover the tire was sliced. Now, he's *really* got a problem. The proper courtesy on a group ride is for the whole group to stop and wait for the one rider to get back on the road again. I remember flatting on a team training ride one Saturday morning. The rest of the team powered on and left me on my own to catch up once I fixed my flat: Such rude behavior from civilized people! I was so offended that I just turned back and rode home. Okay, offended was only the beginning. By the time I got back to my car, I was fuming MAD! That didn't have the effect I expected. Instead of being concerned about my wellbeing, they didn't even notice I was missing. uncouth!

Don't drop the newbie. I doubt if there is any more demoralizing feeling on earth than being the new guy on an unfamiliar ride, having a bad day, and seeing the peloton disappear over the second hill up ahead. The stranger may just be the one guy who forgot to bring a spare tube. More likely he is a stranger in a foreign land. His being completely lost has a high probability. If he or she is new to cycling, being left behind may be just the key to their giving up. How would you like to be left on the road to find your own way home? Oh yes, they forgot to give you a route sheet too. Some clubs actually assign someone to be tail gunner: to ride at the back and make sure the slowest riders are okay. A couple of years ago I rode Thursday afternoons with a group up on the Cumberland Plateau that refused to drop anyone. At every major intersection the ride leader would stop the ride and wait until everyone caught up. That was a wonderful ride. I need to see if they are still staging that one.

And, take your turn at being the tail gunner. I just hate to see someone fall off the back even if he or she is a friend and a strong rider. I guess I've been in that situation myself all too many times. I've nursed riders back home countless times. I learned a long time ago that if a rider is having a hard day and just can't keep going a word of encouragement and a sympathetic partner is priceless. I do confess that I have broken one of the Ten Commandments—the one about not telling a lie—on a few occasions while helping an utterly exhausted rider back home. You see, once you are bonked and the legs all but refuse to turn the pedals any more, the brain can't comprehend (1) the distance back home and (2) the thought of climbing one more hill. So, I have been known to keep telling the poor soul that "We're only a mile or two from home" or "This is the last hill: it's all flat from here on." Now the exhausted body can accept just one more of almost anything, and "...

PROPER ETIQUETTE PLEASE

the last hill" is doable. If the brain had to confront the truth like it's actually fifteen miles and ten big climbs to go your poor, exhausted charge would brain-lock like one of the patients in the movie *Awakenings*. So that way they do not realize that they are being tricked, but accept "one more...."

Take your turn on the pull: lead the group into the wind. Those that like to sit on the back and take advantage of the draft are called wheel-suckers. It's not a compliment. It sounds rude, but it's an accurate description. Please don't ask how I know that moniker so well. However, at my age I feel like I have earned the right to "sit in" some. Actually, I enjoy setting the pace for the youngsters. They aren't expecting an old guy to pull so strongly: I love it! You don't need to pull for hours on end; a couple of minutes every rotation will do. Now, be courteous and allow—even give permission—for a weak or tired rider to sit in. Your day will come.

By the same token, don't try to ride as fast as you can as soon as you get on the pull. Just keep the same steady pace as the group has been going. I'd like to put a huge rubber band on those guys who get on the pull and then put the hammer down. It's discourteous. It splits the peloton, and no one gets the draft advantage. We've been going at a nice, comfortable eighteen MPH and this Armstrong-wanna-be jumps out at twenty-four!

SADDLE SORE SPIRITUALITY

The first thing that happens is the peloton breaks apart and everyone is now pulling for him or herself. Second, those two really strong guys get fed up with me not keeping the pace with the guy on the solo break, and they jump the line up to the front. Now we have two or three groups instead of one smooth paceline. I just let the guy go off on his own, and I keep a steady pace. Hopefully he will be embarrassed and not do it again. No, he does it every rotation. He usually is oblivious to his leaving everyone behind. He likes the feeling of being the fastest guy on the pull. If you don't want to "just let him go," you could yell some select suggestions to him about his teamwork. I have a great, shrill whistle that usually gets the guy's attention. I often have a couple of suggestions too: you know, said in Christian love.

Eat, drink, and clear your sinuses while you are on the back. Eating and drinking causes you to slow slightly and ride less than a straight line. It's sort of like driving and talking on a cell phone. Do all that when you are not affecting anyone else.

Clearing your nose and throat requires a little more tack for obvious reasons. In cooler weather the sinuses tend to become more active thereby requiring some periodic attention. As newbie riders, we all wanted to behave in a refined manner: civilized. I'm trying to be discreet here, okay? You

PROPER ETIQUETTE PLEASE

will be laughed at if you break out the laced handkerchief or the extra-soft tissue. It doesn't work all that well either. Just turn your head to one side (that's important) and do what comes naturally. Exhale strongly through one side. It's called a snot rocket just in case you wanted to know the proper terminology. Now, you see why you need to be at the back of the pack for this maneuver? Some people will announce an alert at the appropriate time. Your choice.

The unwritten and unspoken gentleman's agreement that seems to fascinate most non-cyclists is that, in cycle racing, it is unsporting to attack a leading rider who has been delayed by misfortune. Misfortune may be a flat tire or other mechanical problem or even a crash. Let's say we have four guys in a race any one of which could win the event and one of them has a flat tire. The other three will not attack until the delayed rider is repaired and back in competition. The eventual winner wants to win fair and square by athletic ability, not someone's bad luck. Once the unfortunate rider gets back up to the main group however, the battle in on again.

In the 2001 Tour De France Jan Ulrich was once again in a nose-to-nose battle with Lance Armstrong when he miscalculated a curve on the descent of one of the Alps mountain stages. Ulrich abruptly disappeared over the edge of the road: a sudden plunge down the steep mountainside. I distinctly remember watching that stage on live television and sitting speechless when Ulrich disappeared. One moment he was sailing downhill at fifty miles per hour and the next he was sailing through the weeds and underbrush down a mountainside: the scenic route. The race commentator, and almost everyone else, thought he was out of the race and most likely seriously injured. No one could survive that sort of a crash. Like a TV comedy, several moments later he emerged from the chasm, covered in dirt and twigs looking more than a little dazed just in time to meet his team car with a fresh bike. He checked all his important body parts, jumped on the bike, and set off to rejoin the race.

That was amazing enough until we note that Armstrong and the rest of the lead pack slowed when they received news of Ulrich's calamity. Racing ceased until the dazed Ulrich torn jersey, ripped shorts, and all rejoined the leaders. Armstrong, as race leader, had dictated that the race be neutralized until Ulrich returned. Once that happened, it was foot to pedal and the race was on in earnest.

Two years later in the 2003 Tour de France Armstrong's generosity was repaid when while climbing the French Alps mountain Col du Tourmalet. A young spectator's bag strap caught Armstrong's handlebar and took him instantly to the pavement. Ouch! Nearby, Ulrich along with Tyler Hamilton and two other challenging riders avoided the crash. Hamilton and Ulrich slowed the pace awaiting news that Armstrong had remounted and was able to continue. Ulrich and the others continued to wait until Armstrong reattached to the group, and like in the 2001 race, the battle was on again! Instead of merely finishing the stage and taking overnight to recover; Armstrong regained his composure, attacked, won the stage, and won the tour.

Now, this courtesy applies only to situations of misfortune, not weakness or flawed strategy. We are both savage competitors and gentlemen at the same time.

This all sort of sounds like the two wheeled version of that old story about *"All I Need To Know I Learned in Kindergarten."* I find watching cycling on TV with its code of conduct so refreshing as compared to the usual sit-coms and dramas where deception, lies, and winning at any cost is the norm. I find participating in cycling events even more uplifting with the camaraderie and genuine friendliness of fellow riders.

So, say please and thank you.

The scriptures, both New and Old Testament, are filled with instructions of how man should conduct himself with God and how God agrees to allow man to redeem himself from his sins. If God were in a bike race, he would wait for me even when I fail due to my weakness or flawed strategy. He most certainly waits for me when I have an emotional crash or a physical flat tire. He's going to win anyway. He does like to give us a chance to join him at the podium.

Just look at the Ten Commandments. Sure some of them are stated for us to have a better relation with God. "Thou shalt have no other Gods before me." "Thou shalt not make unto thee any graven image." "Thou shalt not take the name of the Lord thy God in vain." "Thou shalt not accuse Lance Armstrong of using performance enhancing drugs." But some are guidelines to benefit man's relationship to man. "Honor thy father and thy mother." "Thou shalt not kill." That one defiantly enriches associations between us humans. "Thou Shalt not commit adultery." Hmmm. That's not a bad practice either.

Of course we can't talk about relationships without talking about "The Good Samaritan." The Gospel of Luke in chapter 10 outlines Jesus' parable about a man who had come down from Jerusalem on his way to Jericho. This poor soul

PROPER ETIQUETTE PLEASE

could have been a newbie to the Jericho Sunday Morning Club Ride. I think he was probably riding a steel framed Trek. He could have gotten dropped and, since he was from out of town, he surely got lost. No one gave him a Jericho route map, and no one cared if he was dropped. Maybe some bad guys from the Sodom & Gomorrah Cycling Club ran him into the ditch. That club has a bad reputation you know. Could he have flatted his left sandal and didn't have any leather patches in his saddle bag? At any rate he ended up in the ditch; hurt, bleeding, stripped (I'm guessing he ripped his brand new Pearl-Izumi tunic), and left to his own devices. He didn't have any emergency money or a cell phone. Now a preacher came by, probably on his way to teach a Sunday School class and gave the poor, bleeding guy plenty of room by taking to the other side of the road as he whizzed by. Some other riders came by and slowed long enough to have a look at him. They must have determined that he was able to take care of himself as they too went on down the road. Of course they were from the Levite Cycling Team out on a training ride and didn't have time to waste on some out-of-town amateur. Then along comes this guy from Samaria riding solo out for a nice, cool Sunday morning ride. Not only did he bandage the guy's wounds and mend his Pearl-Izumi tunic, but he picked him up and took him to the nearest hospital and paid his ER bill. He made sure the poor guy had a place to stay while he recovered and offered to pay for any additional expenses. WOW! Keep in mind that Jerusalem guys didn't get along at all with Samaritans. They were sort of like Cyclists and dump truck drivers. At the end of this story Jesus said, "Go, and do thou likewise."

Now, I think we have a lot of little lessons to glean from our Samaritan friend over and above the obvious. First, he had the courtesy to stop and see if our poor ditched rider needed any help. Sam must have been on a good roll and didn't actually want to interrupt his awesome training ride: but, he did. Second, he had emergency stuff in his saddle bag and jersey pockets. He may have had the obligatory Snickers Bar. He was riding a "beast" ya know: probably a super light weight custom Italian donkey. He was able to bandage the Jerusalemite's wounds on the spot. Let's just say he had a biblical version of a spare tube and tire tools. He may have even had a leather sandal patch, we don't know. Third, he *gave* our stranger all the stuff he needed. They had no discussion about having the stuff returned or paid for. That's our parable version of "give the guy your spare ... you will need the favor repaid some day." Fourth, Our Samaritan had extra water and race food in

PROPER ETIQUETTE PLEASE

his jersey—ah robe. I wonder if bible time robes had three back pockets. Oh yes, he had an extra Power Bar: Manna flavor. I have a very soft spot in my heart for the fellow rider who notices when I'm out of water and offers some of his. The same goes for Snickers Bars. Fifth, he stayed with our injured friend and didn't just fix him up and take off. In fact he took him the ER and made sure he was taken good care of. Now Sam went a few steps further than even an honorable cyclist goes. He paid for all the repairs, ER bills, and doctors' fees up front. He even left word at check-in that he would pay more if needed. WOW! Oh, I'll give a guy a tube on the road without hesitation or maybe even buy someone a large orange juice and a Snickers Bar at the 7-Eleven, but I've never paid for repairs back at the bike shop. At the end of this parable God said to his disciples, "Go and do thou likewise." That's heavy.

Paul wrote several letters to the Corinthians (we have two of them in the New Testament) about how new Christians should conduct themselves between one another, to God, and to the church. He addressed marriage, parenthood, the government of the church and so forth. He even instructs us on how to conduct worship.

Jesus tells us the parable of the one lost sheep in the Gospel of Luke. The story goes that a shepherd has lost one sheep from of his flock. He goes back and finds the one sheep that was exhausted and got dropped from the group and takes him back to the peloton—ah flock. Everyone is happy. Jesus relates that a "good" shepherd will take care of the one weak member. Isn't that like pacing the weak rider back home from bad day on the road? Jesus said, *"I say unto you, that likewise joy shall be in heaven over one sinner that repenteth, more than over ninety and nine just persons, which need no repentance."* Luke 15:7 Just as you would keep a eye out on a group ride for a weary rider and maybe pace him or her back home, God would have us to keep a spiritual eye open for one another. Do you notice the folks in your Sunday School class and maybe give a phone call through the week to that one soul who looks a little stressed or lonesome? Do you help that unsaved person at work? Maybe that's all it takes to bring him or her into the flock.

In Galatians 6:10 Paul tells us, *"As we have therefore opportunity, let us do good unto all men, especially unto them who are of the household of faith."* Didn't we learn that in kindergarten too? Give a helping hand; be kind to others; say thank you; help a friend in trouble; wave thanks to a dump-truck driver. You see, it all comes down to what Paul told the Galatians. *"7Be not deceived;*

PROPER ETIQUETTE PLEASE

God is not mocked: for whatsoever a man soweth, that shall he also reap. ⁸For he that soweth to his flesh shall of the flesh reap corruption; but he that soweth to the Spirit shall of the Spirit reap life everlasting. ⁹And let us not be weary in well doing: for in due season we shall reap, if we faint not". Galatians 6:7-9 Give a tube, buy someone a cold orange juice and a Snickers, wave to a dump-truck driver and it will always come back to you *"...good measure, pressed down, and shaken together, and running over, shall men give unto your bosom. For the same measure that ye mete withal it shall be measured to you again."* Luke 6:38.

Chapter 10

THE ULTIMATE COMMITMENT

The cycling principle in this chapter may only apply to about half of my readers. In almost all cases this will be the men of the group although I have ridden once or twice with some really unique ladies.

The scriptural truths apply to all of us. You'll see. I'm talking about the cycling tradition of shaving ones legs. See, I told you it applied mostly to men. I know the vast majority of you women riders already shave your legs regularly, so you already have an advantage on us men. You have one leg up on us so-to-speak. Ladies read along; you may get some insight into a not-so-macho tradition and learn a spiritual truth along the way.

Serious cyclists shave their legs. That's just a fact. Go to any major bike race and you will find that most of the male cyclists have just as attractive legs as the girls: often more so. Go to the winner's podium after any serious race and you will not likely find anything more than stubble showing on the lower limbs. Amateur races, newbie races, and Cat 5 events may be quite different as far as clean shaven legs are concerned. At those levels you will most likely find a good crop of well styled leg hair on all but the very best of the category. The newbies have not advanced to the hairless leg level yet.

In the early years of my cycling life my mantra was "I don't ride in the rain, and I don't shave my legs." I was proud of those two positions. I may have said earlier in this book how I hate riding in the rain. The only time I do is when I get caught out and a rogue shower pops up. I study the Weather Channel religiously hours before a ride to avoid any chance that I will get even sprinkled on during a ride. If any chance of a shower appears on the radar I'm burning miles on the resistance trainer in the garage. The first time I rode after having nervously shaved my legs the night before, I got caught in a devilish unpredicted downpour—a gully washer—twenty miles from home. God has a masterful way of humbling His children .

My first cycling event after relocating to the Nashville, Tennessee area I participated in a charity ride out on the Natchez Trace Parkway. The ride had categories for fifty miles, thirty miles, twenty miles and ten miles. I registered for the fifty mile event. It was an interesting ride in that it was sort of a staggered, reverse start. The organizers bused the fifty-mile riders out fifty miles away from the finish line for their starting point, the thirty-milers out thirty miles to their start point and so on. They timed the start of each category so that the fifty mile group would reach the thirties just about the time of their start, and then the two would meet up with the twenties about the time of their start and so on. The idea was rather than have a mass start and everyone eventually spread out and stagger one-by-one to the finish line the starts would be staggered so all the groups finish somewhat together . It was a great idea and worked exceptionally well. The slower, less experienced riders didn't feel demoralized and left off the back of the group immediately off the start . Everyone got the feeling of being important and being part of riding with a large group. The less experienced riders could learn from the now exhausted veterans.

So here I was, the stranger from flatland Florida, setting off on my first event in the Tennessee hills. I was apprehensive about my climbing ability. I took a seat all to myself on the bus just behind a couple of what appeared to be local riders. The ride to the start would be about an hour, so I stretched out my legs across the seat and snuggled against the window for an early-morning snooze on my journey to the start. As the bus trudged along the winding road, I began to hear the conversation from the seat in front of me. I was not eavesdropping, but buses are really no place for private conversations. Now understand that before events, riders usually have some well-orchestrated small talk. It usually goes something like, "Boy, my legs feel like logs today" or "I haven't been getting any good training miles this year" or "I'm just using this for a tune-up ride." You get the idea. All we are trying to do is cover all the pre-excuses in the event of a bad performance today.

As usual I had groomed my legs with my trusty old Gillette the night before the ride. I think I had done a really good job with no noticeable razor cuts: no tell-tell blood-soaked tissue stuck to my skin. I sure didn't want to look unprofessional for my first Tennessee event even if I was unsure of my ability to climb these hills. You see, I had not gotten in any good training miles so far that year, and I was going to use this as a tune-up ride.

I was dozing on and off when the discussion from the seat in front got my undivided attention.

They were talking about the course and who would be strong on the ride today. One fellow said to the other, "I don't think I saw anyone who is all that strong." Hmmm, I wondered where that placed me. The other guy answered (and this really got my attention), " I sure hope we don't have any of those guys with shaved legs. They are WAY TOO SERIOUS." The talk went on to the theme of they didn't like to ride with those "shaved" guys because they took things too resolutely. At that point I sat upright, curled my cleanly shaven legs up under the seat and covered them with my jacket. No use to make enemies on my first ride.

The point is that these two guys respected shaved-legged riders not because of any proof of talent or strength, but on the appearance of being serious and dedicated. They carried themselves professionally and conducted themselves to the nth degree as proper cyclists.

I ended up being the first rider in to the finish that day, and I am still very proud of that. I found that I could climb quite well with the natives. You see, I had the shaved legs advantage. At the finish area festivities I was unashamed of my lily-white, smooth-shaven legs.

When I lived in Florida a team mate and good riding partner vowed never to shave his legs. It just seemed too feminine for him. I, and a few other riders, always teased him about his heavy crop of leg hair. He rode well, but routinely finished seventh or less in races. One Thursday, completely out of the blue, he arrived at the Thursday Night Training Races with bloody, scabbed, and raw but shaven legs. It was a gruesome sight, and it must have been a painful ordeal. But, he was proud of his advancement. He got third that night and continued to finish consistently in the top five for several more years.

So, the question is not "*do* cyclists shave" but, "*why* do cyclists shave; and does shaving really provide a competitive advantage?" Countless magazine articles have been written on why to shave and how to shave. Almost every serious cycling how-to book contributes at least a part of a chapter on the why and how of shaving. Yes girls, we men do need detailed instruction on how to properly shave our legs and how to cope with nicks, cuts, scrapes, and razor burn. But, we men rarely ask women, the experts, how to go about it. It's a macho thing.

So, let's go into some of the reasons why serious cyclists shave our legs.

The first rationale—and the one that is most often offered to naive non-cyclists—is that leg shaving saves weight. Hair doesn't weigh much, but every little bit helps. And, it makes sense.

SADDLE SORE SPIRITUALITY

After all, we try to trim as much weight off our bike components as safely (sometimes *unsafely*) as possible, so why not get rid of that useless hair? Some inexperienced people will believe that one. I always enjoy watching the facial expressions on people when I tell that with a very serious expression. Most people will try to act very intellectual and verbally agree while the subdued facial expression is silently saying "is this guy for real?" Actually the weight saved is so small as to not be measurable. And, if weight were the issue, why not shave the head, arms, and . . . . NO, I'm not shaving the modest amount of head hair I have left. I understand that in some sports, most of the body hair is eliminated. Swimmers, I'm told, go a lot further than we cyclist. I've never done any personal investigation, so I'll have to take others' word on that . Have you ever seen a bearded competitive swimmer? I do like to, in a very serious voice, tell people that saving weight is the reason I shave. You'd be surprised how many people, trying to act very intellectual, buy that one. Try it sometime; you will get some very serious and interesting reactions.

Another good reason to shave is wind resistance. Hair, believe it or not, creates wind drag and thus robs power. After all, all those follicles grouped together grab some serious amounts of

THE ULTIMATE COMMITMENT

atmosphere. However, if that is the case why not shave the arms and head? Good question. In fact all hair does create a wind grabbing effect and does create a certain amount of measurable drag. Well, as it turns out the leg hair robs a great deal *more* power because it is in motion. Let's think about it. The arms and head are just going along for the ride. Wind passes over those areas with a slight amount of drag. Head hair is generally so thick that the passing air tends to flow over it rather than through it, and it is usually covered by a helmet anyway. Chest hair is covered with a jersey negating any follicle drag at all. Arm hair is a little more problematic. I don't even want to discuss beards. Notice, though, that very few serious cyclists have beards. I did ride with a girl from Alabama once that . . . . I'll not go into that. Bradley Wiggins has some serious burns, and he rides quite well.

Legs on the other hand are not only riding along; they are in a constant circular motion too. The air resistance passing over the legs is negligible but magnified immensely because of the travel up and down and fore and aft thus grabbing several times more air than static hair that is only hitching a ride with the bike. The legs are encountering air drag in the forward travel as well as the up and down travel in addition to the static travel derived from the movement of the bike. Not only that, but the speed of the legs in relation to the rest of the body is much faster as each leg moves forward from the nine-o'clock pedal position to the three-o'clock position. Faster equals more drag on those pesky little follicles. The legs create much more movement than other body parts resulting in much more drag simply because of their motion to rotate the pedals. Just sit on your indoor, stationary trainer and pay attention to the amount of air rushing through your leg hair. It's a lot. Compare that to the air passing through your other haired skin: not so much. This theory makes much more sense than the weight-of-the-hair theory. You can get your non-cyclist friends involved in quite a serious conversation with this elucidation.

The following reason makes even more logical sense. Serious riders and certainly professional racers get routine, daily, massages. The legs, for obvious reasons, get the most concentrated attention during the massage. I don't care how good the masseuse or masseur is, rubbing over long leg hair day after day can get painful. So, a much more practical reason for shaving is to reduce pain during massage. The arms are not often the target of the massage and the head is definitely not a target. Unfortunately, most us are cash-strapped having spent all our money on alloy wheels and Spandex leaving very little discretionary cash for massages. But, we attempt to emulate the professionals, so shave we do, even without the daily, professional massage.

I use a great little device called The Stick for routine, after-ride, do-it-yourself leg massages. The Stick is a tough, plastic bar with handle grips on each end and plastic rollers along its length. Rolling The Stick up and down sore leg muscles relieves aching, damaged tissue and is a great and inexpensive substitute for a skilled rub down. However, pesky leg hair can find its way between those pain-relieving plastic rollers, and the rollers tend to pull it out with no regard to your comfort level. Shaving is a must, even for low tech massages.

One more good reason to shave deals with the pain issue also. If you ride very long at all you will have an intimate meeting with the pavement once in a while. Your acquaintance with the road does not necessarily need to be dramatic or involve a visit to your local ER. Most falls are very minor but very embarrassing. A couple of months ago I fell at a stop sign simply because I was daydreaming and forgot to shift down for the deceiving incline before a stop at an intersection at a busy highway. I tried to shift too late and all

SADDLE SORE SPIRITUALITY

I managed to do was roll the chain off the front ring. With no power and almost at a complete stop I met the asphalt knee first followed by the hip while my lower leg tried to chew up the front chain ring. The front chain ring won. All I got was a little road rash and a lot of embarrassment. I never, never fall without someone seeing me. One minute I'm Mr. Cool on my super light weight carbon bike wearing my fancy logoed jersey and the next moment I'm wallowing around on the street like a wino trying not to look like a fool. Of course the driver has to stop and ask if I need help. The answer is always no: always. "No thank you, I'm fine." Well, that little road rash required some first aid and a bandage for several days. The legs are an awful place to get an injury. Hairy legs are no region to place and replace sticky bandages. Ouch! Ouch twice a day for a week. Ouch twice a day for two or three weeks for us diabetics. The other problem with road rash or any injury for that matter is the hair is a great place for germs to hide. Germs inhibit healing. Ouch for two weeks now. So, another (and I think the best reason) for shaving is better healing in inevitable case of injury.

So why not shave the arms too? Well, if you fall, your knees, hips, and/or calves will always get some damage. Usually if you fall; your shoulders, forearms and hands get hit too. However, rarely will you skin the tops of your hands or the tops of your forearms. The bottom parts seem to take the majority of the damage. That leaves the hairless area of the arms, shoulders, and the palms of your hands. I know; occasionally the forearms will get some of a crash but, that is so rare as to make it a non-argument. Okay?

Well, these are a few of the qualified reasons for the traditional leg shave. Some are a little tongue-in-cheek, some are credible. The massage is reliable for the most serious: the pro riders and those of us with very sympathetic spouses. The road-rash issues are certainly valid for many. But the question remains, "is leg shaving necessary or even advantageous for most cyclists?"

In all my years of cycling, I still have not read or heard a really convincing reason either physiological or mechanical supporting the tradition. Oh, the massage reasoning has its merits, but I'm not convinced that is a compelling reason for all but the professional rider. The medical/road rash angle has creditability, but again why restrict it to only the legs? The real answer is no one has a real answer. We just do it. It's tradition. I suppose shaving had some very legitimate purposes in the early days of cycling say way back before the decade of the 90s.

SADDLE SORE SPIRITUALITY

My own personal opinion, and I believe the most valid, is that shaving ones legs is an sign of commitment. It is an outward sign that we (men) are serious and totally dedicated to our sport. I understand that this makes no logical distinction to our lady cyclists. To men however, shaved legs can be an invitation to ridicule and may likely bring on doubts of masculinity. At best it invites strange looks from the uneducated and perhaps incorrect and embarrassing conclusions from others. Clean legs to some equals deviant masculine behavior: incorrect, but it happens.

So why risk the ridicule, the ogling, the awkward questions? Because within the cycling community it is a symbol of commitment. It is a badge of dedication and lifestyle to the sport. It tells other cyclists and non-cyclists that "I am a *real* cyclist. I am fully involved. No matter what I have to do, I will be a complete cyclist." "The opinions of non-shavers do not matter. I am confident in my dedication." Believe me, when a man takes razor to legs, it is the ultimate step of dedication.

As with my friend who started placing four positions higher in races after he started shaving his legs I think it is more psychological than physical. His conditioning did not change. He did not magically get stronger in a day. His skill

THE ULTIMATE COMMITMENT

certainly did not magically become enhanced. His focus changed. He committed.

Remember the two guys on the bus before my first event in Tennessee who were critical of riders who shave. They did not converse about the conditioning advantage of better riders. They did not compare and contrast the strength or skill of other riders. They respected the commitment and dedication of clean-legged riders. It indicated that a shaved rider had the focus to train, to eat properly, to condition his body and mind to accomplish excellence in that one sport. It indicated that a shaved rider is concerned about the most minute detail needed to attain excellence. To them, Clean shaven legs proved it.

Even though I no longer compete, I find myself at endurance, charity, and recreational rides checking out guys legs. Let me rephrase that. I find myself checking out who shaves and who does not. I key in on the ones who shave because I strongly suspect that they are the very serious riders. If the ride becomes competitive I want to know who to keep in check. If the road gets challenging, I want to know who to depend on to follow in a paceline at twenty-eight miles per hour or up a steep climb at six miles per hour. If I am riding in a tight group wheel to wheel and knuckle to knuckle, I want to know who to trust or conversely who to keep at a safe distance. Shaving is an outward sign of an inward commitment.

Living a Christian life in an ungodly world requires a phenomenal amount of commitment. Sin does not take a great deal of self control. Sin generally does not bring on negative judgment from strangers.

In Genesis Chapter 17 God formed a covenant with Abram (whom he named Abraham in this same chapter). God sets the foundation of Israel and the Jewish people and in turn the Christian faith. That covenant involved an extremely agonizing act as far as Abraham viewed it. God Said, *"¹⁰This is my covenant, which ye shall keep, between me and you and thy seed after thee; Every man child among you shall be circumcised. ¹¹And ye shall circumcise the flesh of your foreskin; and it shall be a token of the covenant betwixt me and you. "* Genesis 17:10-11. Oh! Now that's a commitment.

So why did Abraham go through with this? Well, God had promised that Abraham would be the father of a great nation if he agreed to the covenant. Okay. But, Abraham was already a rich and powerful man and an old man. He really had not much to gain except a son which he desperately wanted. But, even with the promise of a son, Abraham had doubts. After all he and

THE ULTIMATE COMMITMENT

Sarah both were pretty old: Sarah especially. He did it as an ultimate commitment to his God. He did it as a total dedication to his God. He was a full believer even unto circumcision. Not only that, but he committed all his posterity to the same ritual and dedication.

Circumcision in those days was an extreme undertaking. I'm quite sure they didn't have surgical grade steel for the procedure. Anesthetics wouldn't be invented until the mid-1800s. OUCH! Now a man had to be absolutely committed to his God to go through with that. Lots of blood and pain was involved which lasted for days.

Circumcision is discussed throughout the Bible in both the Old and the New Testaments. According to the Christian faith circumcision is no longer required: Jesus saved us from the sacrifices of the Law. But, many Christians still hold to the principle if not the act. Why? Because circumcision is a symbol of complete release of self to God. It is total commitment. It is of the heart more than of the flesh. As Paul wrote to the Romans, *"[29]But he is a Jew, which is one inwardly; and circumcision is that of the heart, in the spirit, and not in the letter; whose praise is not of men, but of God."* Romans 2:29

Paul also told the church at Philippi, *"For we are the circumcision, which worship God in the spirit, and rejoice in Christ Jesus, and have no confidence in the flesh".* Philippians 3:3

Does circumcision in and of itself make a man a better spiritual being? Seems not. Does leg shaving make a man a better cyclist? No. They both involve sharp objects near very sensitive areas. They both involve the spilling of blood—maybe in the same amounts. They both involve cutting off seemingly unnecessary parts. They both involve a period of healing. They both tell the world that a complete commitment has been made.

In modern Christianity the act of circumcision is not generally practiced for religious purposes. However the act of living a Godly life should be. Just as the clean-shaven rider elicits respect from other riders, a cleanly-lived life elicits a spiritual respect from other people. Clean legs are symbolic of a dedicated, knowledgeable, and committed rider. A clean, sprit-filled lifestyle is symbolic of a dedicated, knowledgeable and committed Christian.

Paul wrote to the Christians in Rome: *"[1]I beseech you therefore, brethren, by the mercies of God, that ye present your bodies a living sacrifice, holy, acceptable unto God, which is your reasonable service.[2] And be not conformed to this world: but be ye transformed by the renewing of your mind, that*

THE ULTIMATE COMMITMENT

ye may prove what is that good, and acceptable, and perfect, will of God." Romans 12: 1-2

When I go to a new group ride, I look for those riders with blood seeping from fresh razor cuts. When I go to church, social gatherings or into the workplace I look for the blood of Jesus seeping from the spirits of others. How do I see the blood? It's in their ethics. It's in their behavior on the sports field. It's in their language. It shows in their compassion. It's evident in their discernment. It's in their choices of how they conduct their everyday lives. Their lifestyle is symbolic of their commitment to our Lord. Commitment shows in how much we are willing to forego worldly concessions for total commitment to Christ.

Who do you want to follow closely in a fast paceline? Who do you want to partner with on a three mile mountain climb? Who do you want to be elbow to elbow with in a twenty-rider pack at thirty miles per hour? You guessed it: the dedicated and prepared rider. Who do you want to follow into a business agreement? Who do you want to follow you into a business situation? Who do you want to help you through a tragic episode in your life? Who do you want to lead your Sunday school class or your childrens' youth group? My guess is that you want a sold-out, dedicated, prepared Christian who shows the razor burn of commitment.

To whom and to what are you committed? I'm certain you will find peace and joy when you shave off the leg-hair of worldliness and proclaim that you are totally committed to Christ.

Chapter 11

RIDE LIKE A CHAMPION TODAY

As I write this chapter the days are getting shorter, and the air is getting colder. The start of the college football bowl games are only a few days away and my off season regimen has begun. The regular schedule season has ended, and It's been a long and remarkable football year. From my standpoint it has produced some extreme highs and some deep disappointments. Now, I am not really a college football aficionado. I do not closely follow all the conferences, teams or standings: well, okay maybe the standings. I have, however, fervently followed one team for most of my adult life. I was born and raised just a few miles from its well-recognized campus. That school has a produced some of the greatest games in the history of college sports and has a football history, heritage and tradition matched by none.

About twenty-five years ago their newly hired coach with his eyes on a national championship had a sign created with his simple message that would sum up what he expected of his players for every game. It was meant to motivate the players to perform at their very best mentally and physically each and every time they entered the arena. He placed it at the bottom of the stairway exiting the players' locker room so that before every game and before every practice they would see it and carry out its importance. Players since have gained inspiration from its message and carry on the tradition of slapping that sign as they leave the locker room on their way to every game and every practice. That sign says it all, and it has inspired every team, every player and countless fans since. It has become a trademark motto for the athletics and the academics of the university. The five simple words are symbolic of excellence of character. It simply reads, "Play Like A Champion Today." Even if I did not support that team, I would respect that symbol of motivation, dedication and excellence and try to incorporate that message into my own daily life.

So, by now many of you are scratching your heads and wondering how could Bob be a cyclist and a football fan; the two just don't seem like a good match. Those sports have almost nothing in common with the exception perhaps of pain. And the next obvious question is what in the world does this coach's motto have to do with cycling. Attitude may not guarantee success; but lack of an affirmative, dedicated and champion-like approach will almost always hamper the best possible outcome: full success. The better your approach to anything in life the better the result will be, including cycling.

Now back to cycling. A few years ago I had a very close friend spend two or three weeks with me before we set off on a two-day charity ride in some very challenging terrain with one monster mountain climb at the end of the first day. Otherwise a great athlete and a fierce competitor he had not been cycling long, and he was not familiar with the roads and traffic in Middle Tennessee. As a result, he was just a little timid on our first few training rides. He was a good rider and strong, but subtly a little unsure of himself in strange surroundings just like all of us would be. Well, I suppose I should understand that most people are so intimidated by riding with me that they are somewhat ill at ease at first. What do you mean you don't believe that? Okay, no one believes that, and I have yet to find anyone intimidated by me or my riding.

He rode well and strong. He was doing nothing outwardly wrong. He was wisely getting used to our roads, traffic and terrain. In short he was an exceptionally good technical rider.

After the first couple of rides I noticed that we were encountering some motorists who seemed not all that eager to share the road. That's unusual here in Wilson County. Cars were crowding us on the lane when normally they would give us a fair portion of the road. The occasional impatient driver would give a tap on the horn, you know, to just sort of let us know he or she was passing: very courteous. Okay, the occasional impatient driver would give a blast like the Queen Mary coming into port! Every so often someone would shout words of encouragement out of a passing window. Bellow was more the tone and the words are not in good taste to be repeated in a book like this: colorful Tennessee colloquialisms. These were things I was just not accustomed to experiencing since I had moved to Middle Tennessee: Northwest Florida maybe, but not Tennessee. I was embarrassed for the behavior of my fellow Tennesseans in front of my guest. I checked with The Weather Channel to see if we were in a full moon phase. I even checked with Al Gore to see if we were on some accelerated global contamination alert. Nothing.

As we continued to ride the insults occurred less frequently, and courtesy gradually returned over a few days. By the end of my friend's stay we could ride for hours with the respect common among Tennessee drivers.

I look back through my own cycling development years and I can trace a direct correlation between my evolving from my Phread years and the respect I garnered then and the respect I receive from others now. I thoroughly understand that knowledge and skill play a great part in that. Still for many years I have been puzzled about why I was disrespected in the early years and not later on when I am essentially doing the same thing in relation to my interaction with other road users. I have always been respectful of other vehicles on the roadways. Something is different now. What is it?

Yes, I know I have abandoned the knee socks, the T-shirt, the awkward seating position, the imitation leatherette bar covering and so on and so on. That may have brought on some amused teasing from motorists and other riders, and I acknowledge that. But, aside from the obvious technical improvements, I have always ridden on the right edge of the road and obeyed traffic rules. In other words, my interaction with others has not essentially changed.

Too, I well remember my first racing event. It was the Tour De Junque (Tour de junk) in Virginia Beach, VA. The local bike club put on a really fun race day meant to encourage rank amateurs like me. The entry fee was a donation of any bike related item. People brought everything from gear sets to tires and tubes: cheap tires and tubes. Prizes were the winners selection of any of the entry fee items on the table. First place got first pick. Second got second pick and so on. Trophies, given in addition to prizes, were old components mounted on a wood plaque backing. I placed third in my event and won a water bottle along with a trophy made of a mangled, old rear derailleur on a wooden plaque. I still have both carefully stored away in a treasure box in the attic. Everyone had a great time and gained valuable racing skills.

Oh, I practiced and trained until I thought I was a sure winner. I was convinced the pro scouts would be there to discover the likes of someone as talented as me. I had studied all the proper race tactics. I had a real, tight-fitting race jersey and a brand new Vetta helmet. Oh yes, Vetta was state of the art in helmets in those days. I was ready!

I did all the right things from the start. God had provided a strong north wind that day. Oh, I thought that was great! These other novices would not know how to deal with that. I would be the

RIDE LIKE A CHAMPION TODAY

perfect textbook example of pulling with a backwind and drafting with the headwind: so clever!

The only thing was that for all my knowledge and preparation I could not outride two guys who took the lead from the outset and kept it for ten long miles. My strategy fell apart when I ended up pulling into that deadly north wind as well as the tailwind. Everyone else was quite willing to let me do the work. I still to this day don't know how that happened. By early in the race, after the two had ridden out of sight, five of us had formed a small breakaway and were challenging one another for third place. By the last lap, I was exhausted. With about half a lap to go I managed to go off the front and stayed there to clinch third place. I had won my sprint if not the race by a convincing margin.

By my next race, which was in Pensacola, I had improved dramatically. I was the guy to beat that time. To this day my good friend Terry and I argue over who was dead last. I am sure Terry beat me by several yards and he insists he was last.

My early days of regular riding and training brought much disrespect. As with my friend from earlier in this chapter, I was the recipient of many horns and bad-natured cheers. God did protect me from any physical disaster; I have only had one contact encounter with a motor vehicle over all these years, and that was very insignificant.

That lack of respect is sort of hard to put my finger on specifically. Sometimes it was in the form of horns and howls. People seem to have loved to shout "get off the road!" I've always been curious how they figure that is going to influence my riding. I've learned over the years that a faction of motorists exist who do not possess any logic whatsoever.

However, as I gained experience and confidence gradually those unpleasant encounters faded. For the past many years I have experienced very few disagreeable situations out on the road. I can remember in the early years when a conflict with a motorist was a daily occurrence. It was a remarkable day when no disagreement was encountered. Now, just the opposite is true. An unpleasant episode on the road is so rare that it upsets me for days. I keep pondering my memory to see if I had actually done anything to bring on the altercation. Generally not: most likely it is an encounter with one of those factions possessing no logic to their actions.

I've sort of taken notice that the less experienced, more novice riders seem to have the most problems even though they generally do nothing overtly to antagonize other road users. Actually, most novice riders are overly courteous. I've come to the conclusion that the difference is not talent nor experience but attitude. I'm not talking about an arrogant sort of smugness , but about an attitude of confidence that I am riding correctly and courteously. When I and most of my experienced friends ride we generally ride with a great deal of that sort of confidence. We have been on every type of road, in every traffic condition, and encountered every type of motorist possible. We survived! We know our abilities. We know our rights on the roadways, and we respect others' rights. We are confident.

I have no idea what to call that attitude, but I know it exists and it commands respect on the road. Remember my friend who came for the charity ride. He did not change his riding technique, but at the end of his visit, we attracted no more horns or shouts or close encounters of the road kind. He gained confidence and gained the attitude that he belonged on the road.

The closest thing I can associate this phenomenon with is dogs. Dogs can sense fear and frequently will attack when they smell fear in a prey. I'm convinced motorists have the same primal instinct. Novice cyclists, cyclists in unfamiliar surroundings, and cyclists that have never gained a firm understanding of their rights of the road emit some sort of inaudible, invisible, and intrinsic signal to motorists much the same way frightened people do with dogs. Motorists seem to attack the same way dogs attack. Motorists can smell fear in cyclists. Take notice when you are driving of how some motorists will try and intimidate drivers who slightly appear to be apprehensive in traffic situations. Quite often aggressive drivers will bully shy motorists for no apparent reason. I think they smell fear in the timid driver. I'm convinced that is what happened with my friend and me the first few days we trained here in Tennessee.

Racing contains similar instincts. Veteran racers possess an inner-confidence and ride as if they are winners. They have the knowledge to race well, but they also have that instinct to know when the competition is fearful. Veterans know when the less experienced competitor will not commit to attack and they take full advantage. They take full advantage and strike. Good, strong, well prepared, young racers fail because they lack confidence and attitude, not skill or strength. Okay, then there's me, but I have a whole other set of problems to deal with. I have lots of confidence. I'm beaten by many other factors. At times I feel like Rocky Balboa running into Apollo Creed's fist. Rocky had attitude and absolutely no fear!

So, my point is, when you are out on the bike;

RIDE LIKE A CHAMPION TODAY

Ride Like A Champion Today! Apollo Creed would have said it another way; "have the eye of the tiger." You are good. You have every right to be on the road. You have good, well maintained equipment. You know the rules of the road. You even have alloy wheels. Now, go ahead and take your rightful place on the road or in the race and Ride Like a Champion Today!

When you ride with a sloppy T-shirt, running shoes, an ill-fitting helmet, and imitation leatherette bar covers you look like road-prey and you will be treated as such. Put on your proper riding jersey, spandex shorts, proper helmet and ride like you belong. You will get the respect you deserve. You know the rules of the road. You know you have every right to be there. Take possession of your portion in the lane and it will be respected. Ride with authority.

Maintain eye contact with motorists. When you look behind to see approaching vehicles, look drivers in the eye. Give them that look that communicates that you know what you are doing and that you expect them to act appropriately. When you see a driver approaching from a side road or an entrance, look the driver firmly in the eye and keep that eye contact. Be in command of your position. I have observed that when I maintain that direct eye contact motorists often will return the look and gesture in some way that they see me and give me my right of way. Oh yes, I do occasionally get other gestures from out-of-state drivers.

Hold your line. Ride in a path that is true and predictable. When cyclists weave and wander on the road, motorists don't know what the rider is doing or about to do. That creates confusion, frustration, and anger. A champion rides in a true, straight line and maintains position, speed, and direction.

When you change lanes or make a turn, signal and look. Make sure other people on the road know what you are doing. I use my right arm stretched out and my finger pointed to signal right turns. Left turns are signaled with the left arm and finger. I often jab my arm to emphasize my intention. I want drivers to know what I'm doing. Drivers appreciate it. Drivers today usually do not have a clue on earth what the left-arm-pointed-over-the-head-to-the-right means. That's a signal whose time has long passed. When the shoulder narrows or disappears, point and signal that you are merging into the main lane. Don't assume the driver will recognize that situation.

The same etiquette holds for group riding and racing. Let the other riders know your position and your intentions. A simple "on your left/on your right" prevents massive amounts of road rash. Hold you pace too. Nothing is more annoying and dangerous than speeding up, slowing down, speeding up. . . . Keep doing that and you will find you are not invited to the next ride.

Know the rules of the road better than the average motorist. If you know what your rights are, you automatically ride with more confidence and a better attitude. One excellent resource is a book by Bob Mionske JD. titled "Bicycling & The Law." Moinske goes in depth on the rights and responsibilities of both motorists and cyclists. Knowing your lawful rights and how the legal system looks at cyclists is a big boost to your confidence.

I'll bet you feel better, more confident, and have a sky-high attitude already. Now go put on your proper riding shorts and jersey, helmet, check your bike over, air your tires and RIDE LIKE A CHAMPION TODAY!

By the way, that football coach who came up with the "Champion" slogan went on to win a national championship and is regarded as one of the great coaches in football history.

So what does "Play Like A Champion" mean? How do champions play? I'm not sure a specific definition exists, but I think I can list a few characteristics that may identify some behaviors of a champion. For a start they must strive to do their very best all the time. They don't tolerate their own mistakes well. I'd suspect that they practice relentlessly. They honor their sport by behaving honorably both on and off the playing field. They strive to improve their performance continually. They go over each aspect of the game and of their position in the game. I'd suppose they learn from mentors—coaches. They give one hundred percent at every practice and every game. They are totally dedicated to their sport.

Our Christian life is much like a sport: say, a sport like cycling. Lots and lots of practice will be essential and enjoyable. If you are properly prepared to ride with the skills you have learned and respect the rules of the road (the world) and of the peloton (the Christian family) and live diligently, chances are you will win and you will enjoy your life. You will overcome all the obstacles and dangers out there in life and have joy doing it. You will be a champion. *"... I am come that they might have life, and that they might have it more abundantly."* John 10:10

God gave us a Bible full of training advice—coaching if you will—to get us through the game of life on earth and on to the ultimate goal of eternal life with HIM. In one of the earlier chapters I suggested reading some books on cycling and keeping up with the sport by reading magazines. No doubt by now all of you have a shelf full of rather expensive cycling publications by a variety of impressive authors. Where's your Bible? I'll admit that I sometimes find some passages hard to relate to. God foresaw the problem and gave some scholars the ability to construct study Bibles that explain what the passages are really saying and even reference other similar passages. He gave us concordances and Bible dictionaries. Now with the internet, our reference library is limitless. While Paul was in prison awaiting his execution he wrote Timothy, and in 2 Timothy 2:15 he said, *"Study to shew thyself approved unto God, a workman that needeth not to be ashamed, rightly dividing the word of truth."* A champion studies his craft. A champion Christian studies his faith.

Additionally, Paul wrote several letters (books of the New Testament) instructing churches and individuals how to follow God's way. As Christians He has instructed us to study the scriptures with intensity.

Even Christ Jesus when He was led into the wilderness to be tempted of Satan (Matthew 4) defeated all of those ploys by knowing the scriptures. Well, I mean after all He is "The Word." But non-the-less he countered all of Satan's enticements by answering "It is written. . . ." Satan cannot stand against the Word of GOD! Quote The Word back to the devil, and he can't triumph.

He gave us a whole peloton of flesh and blood coaches: preachers, pastors, deacons, elders, counselors, teachers, good friends, Godly parents and the list goes on. Just like we learn cycling techniques from more experienced riders, we learn spiritual proficiency from these gifted coaches. Just like cycling advice though, not every piece of spiritual advice applies to each individual. Most does, but be careful that the advice is for you. You have to search your soul and see if it applies to you and your situation and then try it to see if it in fact works for you. I've found occasionally that people will pass on spiritual counsel to me when in fact The Holy Spirit meant it for them. It was good advice; it just overshot its intended target.

Knowing the rules is a primary part of any sport or game. Without these rules, some written and some simply accepted as proper behavior, the game would be chaos. Imagine if we had no traffic rules. Well, actually, I have been in some parts of the world where *if* traffic rules exist they are completely ignored. Some U.S. states come to mind with that thought too, but I won't mention names. I suspect that in Italy traffic rules went out with the chariot, or maybe Italian traffic rules continue from the days of the chariot. I'm convinced that eye contact between Italian drivers is a sign of weakness and that the horn is actually a substitute for regulations. The loudest horn has the right of way, and no one eyeballs anyone else on the road. Eye contact constitutes a loss of position in the pandemonium of tiny cars and lumbering trucks. Oddly enough, bicycles are given ample consideration. Cyclists give no eye contact either. Inexplicably enough, Italian taxi drivers are able to get their fares to their destinations reasonably safe.

God, however, is not in the chaos business; and he does not want us to be either. Paul tells the Church at Corinth, *"For God is not the author of confusion, but of peace, as in all churches of the saint."*.1 Corinthians 14:33The ultimate rule book, training manual and guide is of course the Ten Commandments.

> *[1]And God spake all these words, saying,*
> *[2]I am the LORD thy God, which have brought thee out of the land of Egypt, out of the house of bondage.*
> *[3]Thou shalt have no other gods before me.*
> *[4]Thou shalt not make unto thee any graven image, or any likeness of any thing that is in heaven above, or that is in the earth beneath, or that is in the water under the earth.*

⁵Thou shalt not bow down thyself to them, nor serve them: for I the LORD thy God am a jealous God, visiting the iniquity of the fathers upon the children unto the third and fourth generation of them that hate me;
⁶And shewing mercy unto thousands of them that love me, and keep my commandments.
⁷Thou shalt not take the name of the LORD thy God in vain; for the LORD will not hold him guiltless that taketh his name in vain.
⁸Remember the sabbath day, to keep it holy.
⁹Six days shalt thou labour, and do all thy work:
¹⁰But the seventh day is the sabbath of the LORD thy God: in it thou shalt not do any work, thou, nor thy son, nor thy daughter, thy manservant, nor thy maidservant, nor thy cattle, nor thy stranger that is within thy gates:
¹¹For in six days the LORD made heaven and earth, the sea, and all that in them is, and rested the seventh day: wherefore the LORD blessed the sabbath day, and hallowed it.
¹²Honour thy father and thy mother: that thy days may be long upon the land which the LORD thy God giveth thee.
¹³Thou shalt not kill.
¹⁴Thou shalt not commit adultery.

¹⁵*Thou shalt not steal.*

¹⁶*Thou shalt not bear false witness against thy neighbour.* ¹⁷*Thou shalt not covet thy neighbour's house, thou shalt not covet thy neighbour's wife, nor his manservant, nor his maidservant, nor his ox, nor his ass, nor any thing that is thy neighbour's."* Exodus 20:1-17

In addition and even more directly, Jesus himself gave us some very specific guidelines for life in his parables and sermons recorded in the New Testament. I sorta like the passage in **the Gospel of John, Chapter 8 where He tells the** scribes and Pharisees, *"He that is without sin among you, let him first cast a stone. . . ."* I like it best when I am the one about to be stoned.

Too I think that competitors, athletes, great cyclists—champions—learn to conquer fear. I'm sure they have fear, but they have learned to conquer fear and the effects of fear. Soldiers are much the same. They do what is necessary in spite of fear. *"There is no fear in love; but perfect love casteth out fear: because fear hath torment. He that feareth is not made perfect in love."* 1 John 4:17-19

In 1990 I entered my first race after having broken my right femoral neck in a cycling accident. That's the ball that connects the leg to the hip. I had immediate surgery followed by ten months of healing and rehabilitation. My doctor reluctantly told me I could ride, but if I fell I would do irreparable damage to that hip.

As you may construe, racing at that point was not the brightest thing I could have done on a springtime Saturday morning. I should have stayed home and cut the grass or something more domestic rather than racing with a bunch of amateurs who had been shut in all winter. I may not be bright, but I am zealous. I should tell you that I am not brave either. Interstate 10 has seven exits between Pensacola, Florida and Mobile, Alabama; and I very nearly turned around at each one and headed back home. The lawn mower had more appeal at every exit ramp. Even at the event in downtown Mobile I had strong thoughts of being a spectator and not a participant. I overcame the fear and actually won that race.

Facing a particularly hard climb can bring on fear bad enough to send us packing back home too. The thought of the pain alone is bad enough. But, the thought of having all those "good" climbers ride past while we are walking uphill in cleats is a powerful dread. More fearful yet is the thought of going DOWN a steep and fast decent. One little misjudgment and it's either over the edge with a quick trip to the ER or sliding all the way down on one's backside. Descending at forty to sixty miles per hour on twisting roads with riders on all sides can bring on white knuckles and cold sweats even before the start. However, because we love the victory of conquering that monster climb, we face it head on. Maybe "head on" was not a good choice of words. Okay, three trips to the port-a-john before the start and a near fall because our feet refuse to click into the pedals is explained away as a ritual before every such event. However, we do it and we are champions. We are champions because we face our fears and do what cyclists do, and we love it.

Fear grips us all. Fear grips us most harshly in our spiritual walk. But, God is not the author of fear as he is not the author of chaos. Scripture has devoted much to teaching us to "fear not" in our spiritual lives.

> " [1]*The LORD is my shepherd; I shall not want.* [2]*He maketh me to lie down in green pastures: he leadeth me beside the still waters.* [3]*He restoreth my soul: he leadeth me in the paths of righteousness for his name's sake.* [4]*Yea, though I walk through the valley of the shadow of death, I will fear no evil: for thou art with me; thy rod and thy staff they comfort me.* [5]*Thou preparest*

a table before me in the presence of mine enemies: thou anointest my head with oil; my cup runneth over. ⁶Surely goodness and mercy shall follow me all the days of my life: and I will dwell in the house of the LORD for ever. Psalm 23

Wow! after reading that again I think I can conquer anything. *"Nay, in all these things we are more than conquerors through him that loved us."* Romans 8:36-38

Paul tells Timothy, *"For God hath not given us a spirit of fear; but of power, and of love, and of sound mind."* 2 Timothy 1:7As the Israelites are about to cross the Jordan and enter the Promised Land, God prepares his servant Joshua for the task ahead. God tells Joshua at the beginning of the book of Joshua; *"Have not I commanded thee? Be strong and of good courage; be not afraid, neither be thou dismayed: for the LORD thy God is with thee whithersoever thou goest."* Joshua 1:9 He (GOD) was not only speaking to Joshua, but through him to the Israelites (the peloton) as well. He is speaking to us. I can imagine a big, gold sign at the entrance to the Promised Land stating "Enter Like A Champion today", and I can see every Israelite slapping the sign as they crossed the Jordan.

RIDE LIKE A CHAMPION TODAY

Remember my writing earlier that I think motorists can smell fear in cyclists like dogs can smell fear in people, and they want to attack? When you ride with confidence that unexplained phenomenon is negated. When we live our daily lives in confidence that God gave us a spirit of power and love and sound mind and that we are more than conquerors through Him the world can sense our confidence and the presence of God over us. They then are afraid to attack. We are living like a champion and the world can smell it.

Of course a good champion is well prepared to take on the game at hand. The champion rider has trained well and is physically ready for the challenge. The champion rider has a well maintained bike, wears the proper shorts and jersey, and wears a helmet and gloves all the time. The champion rider has alloy wheels.

Paul tells the church at Ephesus (and all of us) how to prepare to be champions for the faith.

> "*10Finally, my brethren, be strong in the Lord, and in the power of his might. 11Put on the whole armour of God, that ye may be able to stand against the wiles of the devil. 12For we wrestle not against flesh and blood, but against principalities, against powers, against the rulers of the darkness*

of this world, against spiritual wickedness in high places. ¹³Wherefore take unto you the whole armour of God, that ye may be able to withstand in the evil day, and having done all, to stand. ¹⁴Stand therefore, having your loins girt about with truth, and having on the breastplate of righteousness; ¹⁵And your feet shod with the preparation of the gospel of peace; ¹⁶Above all, taking the shield of faith, wherewith ye shall be able to quench all the fiery darts of the wicked. ¹⁷And take the helmet of salvation, and the sword of the Spirit, which is the word of God: ¹⁸Praying always with all prayer and supplication in the Spirit, and watching thereunto with all perseverance and supplication for all saints; ¹⁹And for me, that utterance may be given unto me, that I may open my mouth boldly, to make known the mystery of the gospel,. . . ." Ephesians 6:10-19

That's how to live like a champion.

And, if a champion rides with the proper knowledge and the proper preparation and the proper equipment and having overcome fear then confidence must follow and become part of that rider. Ride like you belong, because you do.

We can walk through life with confidence and

boldness because we are children of the Living God. That family is infinitely stronger and more powerful and absolutely eternal compared to any cycling club or peloton you could ever imagine. What team director is going to give his own life for you so that you can have everlasting life? None. Jesus did!

Just as we can ride through the streets and roads and look drivers and other riders squarely in the eyes, so too can we walk through our daily lives and look sin and adversity squarely in the eyes and be champions.

Paul wrote to all of us when he wrote to the early Christians in Rome.

"15For ye have not received the spirit of bondage again to fear; but ye have received the Spirit of adoption, whereby we cry, Abba, Father. 16The Spirit itself beareth witness with our spirit, that we are the children of God: 17And if children, then heirs; heirs of God, and joint-heirs with Christ; if so be that we suffer with him, that we may be also glorified together. 18For I reckon that the sufferings of this present time are not worthy to be compared with the glory which shall be revealed in us." Romans 8:15-18

We are joint heirs with Christ! By what greater authority can we walk with heads high through *"...the valley of the shadow of death?"*

Paul also writes the early Christians of the church of Galatia and states, *"⁶And because ye are sons, God hath sent forth the Spirit of his Son into your hearts, crying, Abba, Father. ⁷Wherefore thou art no more a servant, but a son; and if a son, then an heir of God through Christ."* Galatians 4: 6-7

Have you ever met a cyclist, who without even turning a pedal, you know to be a strong and good rider. How? They carry themselves with confidence. They don't have to brag; they know who they are. They behave like a champion.

Have you ever met a person who, without your asking, you just somehow know to be a righteous and Godly person? How about that person that, just somehow, you know you can trust? How do we sense righteousness in some and fear in others? Do you know anyone who seems to have their spiritual life together? They may not be always immune to illness or tragedy in life, but they are able to cope with adverse things and give God the glory. What about those saints who when faced with temptations are able to stand firmly on spiritual truths and walk away from sin's bait? Oh yeah, those folks are not tempted nearly as severely as I am. My guess is that they have studied the Word, put their faith in Christ, put on the full armor of God and walk through life knowing they are an actual child of God. They are Christian Champions. If you have given your soul to God through Jesus Christ , you are a member of His family. You may want to study more. You may want to acquire some more of that "full armor." But, you are a champion. So, as a Christian, Live Like a Champion Today!

Chapter 12

IT'S NOT ABOUT THE BIKE

As you may have discovered reading this book, I love to cycle. Oh, I have had certain periods in my cycling life that I had to take a short break from the saddle. Those days did not last long as I found that I really couldn't stay off the road for a long period. Once I allowed my body to rejuvenate and my mind to refresh I was, as the country song goes, "on the road again."

Oh, certainly, I have experienced a very few times when I thought about giving up my sport altogether. I do experience that feeling more as this body begins to age, and I'm not able to keep the pace with the youngsters like I once did. I did love showing those kids that the old man could make them suffer if they wanted to keep up. The few long-healing injuries that I have experienced brought on some temporary doubts about my desire to continue but recovery brought with it the passion to ride again. I'm recovering from a broken leg bone just now that is a result of a non-cycling accident, and doubts of my returning to the saddle crept into my mind. But, as I progress I am becoming more and more anxious to put foot to pedal and feel the clean, cool morning air rush across my face and feel my lungs beg for oxygen once again. I'm a cyclist.

I believe that cycling has kept me young at heart. I am ashamed to admit that I moderately enjoy letting people know that I still ride twenty to thirty miles a day, and I still climb mountains just for the pure enjoyment of it. Oh I make sure I do it in a tactful, subtle and modest manner. I must pray for forgiveness for my pride. However many of my friends and acquaintances are either riding golf carts for exercise, or they are wearing out the old recliner. I love the idea that I can still play tag with my granddaughters, and I can still impress those youngsters out on the road.

I am confident that cycling too has kept me physically sound even though I am approaching what some may call those golden years. I don't see age as golden: I see myself now as beginning to ripen well. Fruit, if kept properly, can last well beyond its sell-by date. I still have many challenging and happy miles left to travel. The injury I am now recovering from is a fracture of my fibula caused by a evil wet rock that was hiding by a riverbank in West Scotland while I was on a photo shoot on River Orchy. After that brutal granite attack I managed ten more days being a tourist and photographer and then traveled home via three airports before seeking medical attention. I give cycling credit for the physical stamina to accomplish that. (I wrote that in a tactful, subtle and modest manner).

We've had a great journey, me and my bikes. I just can't imagine what I may have missed out on in life had I not experienced precious parts of it from the saddle. And, I am looking forward to many more wonderful miles. I'd like to think that the streets of gold all have well marked bike lanes.

In order for me to enjoy this life on the bike God provided me with the perfect wife and best friend who never once objected to my riding. Although she has no personal attraction to cycling she has been my best fan and loyal crew member for all these years. She has picked me up on lonely roadsides when I had the occasional un-repairable breakdown. She has waited for me in ER waiting rooms anxiously praying for my healing. She nursed my wounds and never scolded me for being so clumsy as to have injured myself in the first place. She has stayed in cafes and motels while I explored alien roads. She has camped out on numerous roadsides and curbsides and cheered me on while I attempted to race. She became a celebrity volunteer at many of the cycling events that I frequented during the years. For several years she was affectionately christened "The Lunch Lady" for the Nashville Tour De Cure charity ride. She allows our home to be the team cafeteria for any of the local riders who need an after-ride snack or a tall glass of cold orange juice. She opens up spare rooms and floor space to racers and riders traveling through and in need of a place to stay for a night or two. God certainly provided me with the perfect wife and best friend.

I hope I have given you the inspiration through this book to explore the great world of cycling. I hope that some of the advice is helpful to you and that it prevents you from making some of the many mistakes that I have made through the years. But, that is not the main objective of my writing.

As enjoyable and rewarding as cycling is; the purpose of this book has been to bring us, me and you, to a closer and more personal relationship with the living God. For me, cycling only emphasizes and reinforces the glory of my God and of His Son, Jesus. The parallels that I have discovered and shared with you apply not only to the saddle, but to everything we encounter and experience in life. God is at the center of all that we are and all that we do. I hope I have opened your mind up to seeing the parallels in everything you encounter.

Just as training, studying, and confidence make cycling more enjoyable a close relationship with God through Jesus makes life itself a joy. John recorded Christ's words in The Gospel of John Chapter 10 verse 10: *"I am come that they might have life, and that they might have it more abundantly.[11] I am the good shepherd: the good shepherd giveth his life for the sheep."*

Before I discovered cycling I had no concept of how joyful it could be. It all began back on the quiet roads of Harrison County, Mississippi in order to save gas money in our overstretched budget. That was motivation enough, but it was only the beginning of a continual lifetime of ever-increasing benefit and happiness. The more I ride, the better it gets.

The same is boundlessly more true with my relationship to God through His Son Jesus Christ. I asked Jesus to save me and to live in my heart—in my soul; my spirit—way back when I was a young boy. That started a personal relationship that has grown and strengthened continually throughout my life. And, just like cycling, the more I give myself to Him the more I get back in peace and abundant joy.

> *"Give, and it shall be given unto you; good measure, pressed down, and shaken together, and running over, shall men give into your bosom. For with the same measure that ye mete withal it shall be measured to you again."* Luke 6:38

Cycling gives joy and benefit even for the casual rider, and it is worth every bit of effort invested. Of course the more you put into it the more you get from it. A personal relationship with God gives joy and a more abundant life. However, like cycling, the more you give to God the more blessings you get back "good measure, pressed down, and shaken together."

But to get any profit you must turn that first pedal. To receive the bounty of a personal bond with God you must first accept his Son, Jesus Christ. "*For God so loved the world, that he gave his only begotten Son, that whosoever believeth in him should not perish, but have everlasting life."* John 3:16 Just as I have asked you to experience the bike, I infinitely more so ask you to accept Jesus Christ as your savior and begin an awesome life: a life you never imagined could be yours.

SADDLE SORE SPIRITUALITY

I know that many who are reading this book have already given their lives to Christ. To you I challenge you to train harder by releasing more of yourself to God. I know the training is not easy, but the rewards are unlimited. Think about the first time you tried riding that big hill. It was daunting. The thought of doing it was terrifying and the effort was immense. But, once you cleared the summit, the feeling was incredible. Then you wanted to do a bigger one with more challenge and an even better reward. Your journey with God is much the same. The thought of giving even more of yourself to our God may be overwhelming, but once you start up that ascent to Him and to His purpose for your life the rewards are out of this world. You have to start though. Once you do, the effort is much easier than you imagined. Jesus spoke as recorded in the Gospel of Matthew: "*[28] Come unto me, all ye that labour and are heavy laden, and I will give you rest.[29] Take my yoke upon you, and learn of me; for I am meek and lowly in heart: and ye shall find rest unto your souls[30] For my yoke is easy, and my burden is light..*" Matthew 11:28-30

God will bring you to the top through His strength. You just have to call on Him. Countless times I have been faced with riding challenges that seemed to be beyond my ability and strength. The Holy Spirit has spoken to my spirit and reminded me of the power in the name of Jesus: just the name. The first time I attempted to ride Monteagle Mountain I became utterly fatigued. My legs were burning like Christmas Yule logs and my lungs were about to burst. I came to a point where I thought I had no more strength to turn a pedal even one more time. I was ready to quit. At that point the Holy Spirit spoke to me and reminded me of the power of the name of Jesus and instructed me, right there half way up the mountain, to speak the name Jesus. "Okay Holy Spirit, I can't breathe; how do you expect me to speak?"

"You are exhaling, so speak on the exhale"

My reluctance to give in to the mountain forced me to consider and obey. I began faintly voicing on each exhaled breathe "Je" and on the next exhale "sus." As much as I wanted to, I couldn't utter the complete name with one breath. But, put the two together and I was calling the name of Jesus. After a couple hundred yards of "Je. . . . . . . .sus" my strength began to return, and I began to be able to faintly say His whole name in one breath: "JESUS." The more I called His name, the stronger I became until I could boldly call out "JESUS!" I still wonder what that young man—the man I passed on the way up—must have thought as I eased past him on a fifteen percent incline faintly panting "JESUS" with each labored breath. There is POWER in the name of the LORD! I still call on His name on monster climbs and at those times when I have overextended myself like at the end of a 100-mile event when I don't think I have the strength to continue. His name, He, has never failed me. *"Forasmuch as there is none like unto thee, O LORD; THOU ART GREAT, AND THY NAME IS GREAT IN MIGHT.:* Jeremiah 10:6

Our God wants us to succeed, and He wants us to have life with joy and abundance. All we have to do is give up self and accept his grace. He is waiting. *"For the mountains shall depart, and the hills be removed; but my kindness shall not depart from thee, neither shall the covenant of my peace be removed, saith the LORD THAT HATH MERCY ON THEE."* Isaiah 54:10

I hope you have enjoyed reading this little conversation I have written on the love of God and the miracle He has given us in cycling. If you never mount a saddle or turn a peddle please give your heart to the loving God. He loves you. Now, bow your head and thank Him for all he is and all he has given. Ask Him to give you strength to accept more and more of Him. Put on the full armor of God, and start climbing that mountain of faith. *"Wherefore seeing we also are compassed about with so great a cloud of witnesses, let us lay aside every weight, and the sin which doth so easily beset us, and let us run with patience the race that is set before us,"* Hebrews 12:1

Next, put on your spandex shorts and jersey. Air up those tires that are mounted on your new alloy wheels. Strap on your helmet and let's go for a ride.

"**²⁸ Hast thou not known? hast thou not heard, that the everlasting God, the LORD, THE CREATOR OF THE ENDS OF THE EARTH, FAINTETH NOT, NEITHER IS WEARY? THERE IS NO SEARCHING OF HIS UNDERSTANDING. ²⁹ He giveth power to the faint; and to them that have no might he increaseth strength. ³⁰ Even the youths shall faint and be weary, and the young men shall utterly fall: ³¹ But they that wait upon the LORD SHALL RENEW THEIR STRENGTH; THEY SHALL MOUNT UP WITH WINGS AS EAGLES; THEY SHALL RUN, AND NOT BE WEARY; AND THEY SHALL WALK, AND NOT FAINT."** Isaiah 40:28-31

GLOSSARY

Cycling words and terms

Arm/Leg warmers: Snug fitting pull-on sleeves/leggings for the arms/legs meant to help keep the rider warm but easily put on or taken off when the weather changes. These are great for cool morning rides when you need something for warmth, but they can be removed easily and stowed in a jersey pocket when not needed. They are great for cold-morning haters like me.

Bar Tape: A cushioning wrap that covers the handlebars. Bar tape provides a good gripping surface and cushions the rider's hands and arms from road shock and vibrations.

Bars: Handlebars. Bars come in several different shapes and materials. Road bikes generally have curved, downturned bars. Mountain bikes generally have straight bars.

Beater bike: An old bike that may not look good but is in sound mechanical shape. Beater bikes are great for rain days when you may not want to take the "good" bike out and get the little darling dirty. Beater bikes are good too for commuting, because a thief might think it is a junk bike and pass it up for your buddy's expensive carbon one.

Bibs: Bibs is short for bib shorts. Bib shorts are one piece riding shorts that have over-the-shoulder suspenders built in. They are sort of like bib overalls for cyclists. Bibs stay in place much better than regular elastic waist band shorts that tend to roll down below fat bellies like...well you know.

Bonk: (Also see Hitting the Wall) bonk or bonking is the total loss of power, energy and strength. The bonk generally occurs when the cyclist is at the furthest point from home and has no more food or water. Bonking is often caused by overextending ones abilities or miscalculating the amount of food and/or water to bring along.

Booties: Foot and shoe covers. Booties are tight-fitting shoe, foot, and ankle covers often used to keep the feet and ankles warm (and/or dry) during cold or rainy days on the bike. Often booties are used by riders for time trial events for an aerodynamic advantage.

GLOSSARY

Brain Bucket: Helmet. Early cycle helmets truly were brain buckets and often brain boilers. The early helmets provided little protection and often caused more harm than help. Today's helmets are light, cool, and offer good head protection. (also see skid lid)

Breakaway: A breakaway (or a break) is a rider or a small group of riders opening up a gap from the peloton. I've rarely actually experienced being in a breakaway, but I have observed many breaks going on up the road.

Bridge: closing the gag that the breakaway has created. A bridge may be accomplished by a single rider or a small group of riders seeking to join the break.

Broom Wagon: The vehicle that sweeps a course picking up stragglers that have no chance of making the finish on their own. Broom wagons are actually very nice to ride in…I've heard.

Bunny hop: The act of making the bike actually jump off the ground in order to avoid some obstacle on the road. Obstacles could be anything from debris on the road to curbs in the event a rider miscalculates a turn. Small dogs and tumbleweeds are counted as obstacles.

Cadence: Pedal speed measured in pedal revolutions per minute.

Cassette: The set of gears at the rear wheel. Cassettes may have up to eleven gears (cogs) and are interchangeable to allow for different demands like terrain or ability. Cassettes are described by numbers relating to the smallest and largest cog in the set such as 12-19 or 11-25. The bigger the large number, the lower the gear ratio which allows for easier climbing. The smaller the small number indicates that gear may be used for greater speed. I need something like an 11-200.

Century: A 100 mile ride completed in one day. A rider's first century ride is sort of a rite of passage like a club initiation where inductees beat themselves into complete submission.

Chainring: The big gear ring(s) on the front. Generally a bike has two chainrings one larger than the other. They are sort of like Hi/low ranges in an off-road vehicle.

Chamois: The padding in the business area of riding shorts. Originally, the so-called padding was simply a thin piece of chamois leather which dried out between rides and caused severe abrasions and discomfort during the first half hour or so of a ride. This discomfort brought about

GLOSSARY

the invention of chamois cream and Butt Butter. Modern shorts have synthetic chamois that is actually well padded and does not dry out between rides. Good ones actually wick moisture away and are quite comfortable.

Cleat: The device attached to the bottom of the cycling shoe that fits into the pedal and holds the foot firmly onto the pedal. The original cleats were simply hunks of hard plastic with a notch cut out that fit into the pedal and was kept in place by a leather strap around the shoe. Mountain bikes sometimes use the same antiquated system. (see clipless pedals)

Clincher: A type of tire that that fits around the edge of the wheel rim with a stiff bead much like a car tire. The Tube is separate and is placed inside the tire. The other main tire type for bicycles is the sew-up. (see Sew up) Clincher tires are the most common for general riding and training since they are easy to change and repair when punctured.

Clipless pedals: Pedals made very much like ski bindings in that the shoe has a cleat that fits into the spring-loaded pedal. Clipless pedals allow the rider to simply step into the pedal to securely attach the foot to the pedal. It also allows the foot to easily and rapidly disengage from the pedal when needed by simply twisting the foot sideways. However, occasionally one will; for some strange, unknown reason, come to a stop and forget how to "click out." This always happens when being observed by a non-cyclist motorist or several adolescent kids nearby. Every rider will fall at least once during the first ride using clipless pedals.

Criterium: Races on a short, closed circuit consisting of several laps. These races are generally referred to as "Crits." Generally, criteriums are staged on city streets and provide some fast and exciting races. Crits require excellent bike handling skills and strong concentration. Crits are most popular in the United States.

Derailer: Derailers are the part of the drive train that make gear changes possible. They move the chain from one gear cog to another. Bikes will have one at the front for the two chainrings and one at the back for changing gears on the cassette. They are both activated by levers on the handlebar.

Domestique: This is the rider who works for and sacrifices for the designated team captain. Domestique literally means "servant" in French. A Domestique brings food, water and anything else needed to the captain or any of the designated

GLOSSARY

leaders on the team during a road race. The Domestique also rides as a pacesetter and protector for the overpaid and lazy captain who takes all the glory and prize money. Domestiques will even give bikes and wheels to the team hot shots when needed, and then they are left standing on the side of the road waiting for the team car. I've been a Domestique.

Down Tube: the slanting frame tube that goes from the head tube to the bottom bracket where the pedal axle is located.

Drafting: The technique of riding closely behind another rider. The rider in front, the rider on the pull, will have to push his/her way through the thick, heavy air while the drafter rides in less wind resistance. Drafting all day and not taking the pull will get you uninvited to the next ride. Really!

Dropped: Being left behind on a group ride or a race: also known as falling off the back. This causes a very lonesome and demoralizing feeling.

Drops: The lower part of the curved, downturned handlebar on a road bike.

Echelon: This is drafting technique used when groups ride with a crosswind. Instead of riding directly behind the rider ahead, in an echelon riders will ride slightly to one side and behind the rider in front forming a diagonal paceline.

Engine: you

Face plant/header: This is a crash were the rider generally goes over the bars, screaming and yelling like a schoolgirl just before making contact with the road: face-first.

False Flat: A false flat is the part of a hill that looks to be flat, but is in fact still rising. It can also be an actual flat plateau between two or more rises on a climb. Both are really demoralizing. The latter may trick the rider into thinking she or he has made the summit, but in fact the cruel mountain has more miserable climbing to go.

Feed Zone: The best section of any road race course. The feed zone is a designated section of the course where teams are allowed to pass food and water to riders. Support staff generally passes items to their riders in satchels called musette bags.

Food Stop/rest stop: This is the feed zone for non-racing long distance events. Food and refreshments are set out for riders rather than passed off as in a racing feed zone. This is the best part of the endurance ride.

GLOSSARY

G.C.: General Classification. This is a list of the accrued times for riders competing in stage races. Naturally the rider with the least aggregate time is the leader and the other riders' times are listed according to how much time they are behind the leader. I find that checking the GC from bottom to top is easiest.

Gear Cluster: The group of gear cogs that make up the cassette. Gear clusters are quoted according to their smallest gear cog and their largest gear cog. Gear clusters may have anywhere from five to eleven gears in the cluster.

Gear inches: Gear inches is the number of inches a bicycle will travel with one revolution of the pedals. This is calculated using a formula incorporating the number of teeth on the chain ring being used, the number of teeth on the rear cluster cog being used, the wheel diameter and the tire size: very academic stuff.

Granny Gear: The combination of the smallest chain ring and the largest rear cog. This combination will give the most power at any given cadence and is used for climbing monstrous hills, enormous mountains, or inclined driveways. Granny gears may get you home once you have bonked twenty miles from home.

Groupo/groupset: A groupo is the components that comprise the drive train and other essential components of the bike. Groupos may include drive train parts only, or they may include brakes, hubs, and other parts as well. Groupos are usually expressed in terms of the manufacturer and model such as Shimano Ultegra or Campy Record. The major suppliers of groupos are Campagnolo (Campy), Shimano, and Sram.

Hammer: To go all out.

Hit the Wall: BONK! It means to completely run out of power, energy and strength. The wall generally hits when the cyclist is at the furthest point from home and has no more food or water. This is generally caused by overextending ones abilities and/or miscalculating the amount of food and/or water to bring along. (See bonk)

Intervals: A training technique wherein a rider puts in an all-out effort for a short but specific duration and then recovers for a reasonable period only to repeat the drill over and over again until utter exhaustion. Other sports may call intervals burst training, but what do they know? At least one coach has instructed his riders that if they don't vomit on the final interval they have not tried hard enough. He's no longer coaching.

GLOSSARY

ITT: Individual Time Trial. The race of truth. This is a time trial by individuals only: no team tactics. See time trial.

Kickstand: A brace attached to the bike frame that holds the bike up while the rider goes for candy and soda. Phread gear. No self respecting rider would ever use a kickstand.

Levers: Used to actuate the brakes and/or shifters. These are the stylish little finger-looking pieces that hang on the front, curved part of the handlebar. Very important gadgets especially when coming to a stop sign at the bottom of a long hill.

Metric: A ride or a race of 100 kilometers sometimes called a metric century. A metric is 62 miles (remember high school science class?). Doing a metric is a way for a rider to truthfully say "I did a hundred" and let people assume they meant miles. It's an easy mistake to make.

Motorpace: A training technique whereby a cyclist will ride closely behind a motor vehicle and take full advantage of the draft. Motorpacing helps with speed, cadence, and power. Vehicles used are usually motorcycles or mopeds, but cars, pick-ups, trucks, vans and buses may be used at one's own risk. It's always a good practice to have the driver's permission before motorpacing. Police often frown on the practice.

Musette: [moo-**zet**] A satchel or bag used to pass food and other refreshment along to a rider during an event.

Off the Back: Way behind the main group or peloton. A lonely location I'm very familiar with.

Off the front: Out in front of the group. A lonely location I'm very unfamiliar with.

On the rivet: A term used to describe a rider performing an all-out speed effort. In order to make a determined speed attack riders will usually move forward on the saddle as much as possible. The term comes from the not-so-recent days when leather saddles were assembled with a large, brass rivet on the nose of the saddle. Riders would move forward until they were riding completely on the nose: on the rivet.

On your wheel: Riding closely in the slipstream of another rider. Drafting. Letting the front rider know your position is considered good etiquette. "(I'm) on your wheel."

Oxygen dept: Your lungs can't keep up with your legs or your ego. You can no longer breathe.

GLOSSARY

Paceline: A group riding in file, one bike's front wheel close the rear wheel of the rider ahead. Riding in a paceline can reduce the energy expended by up to thirty percent.

Pack: the group of riders. Peloton.

Pedaling in squares: The pedaling form that occurs once you encounter the bonk, hit the wall, oxygen debt or just plain fatigue. It's the opposite of Pedaling in circles like when you started out this morning.

Peloton: The large, main group of riders also known as the group, the pack, the bunch or the field. Also known as the fella's we're trying to keep up with.

Phread or **Fred:** The Geeks of the cycling world. Phreads are the most unstylish riders on the road. They also ride with unorthodox form. Many times Phreads do have state-of-the-art equipment and gear, however they rarely use any of it properly. A Wilma is the female counterpart of a Phread.

Potato chipped (wheel): A badly damaged or fatigued wheel. Since bike wheels are under a great amount of stress from the tensioned spokes, once the wheel has been damaged it twists itself into the form of a Pringle.

Presta valve: A European-style tire-tube air valve found on most road bike inner tubes. A small threaded valve-cap on its end must be unscrewed before air can enter or exit. The tire pump connection is not screwed onto the presta valve; it is held onto the valve by a tight-fitting rubber grommet. Presta valves are used on most road bike tubes just to increase the sales of tire pumps.

Prime: Pronounced prEEEEm (go figure) and has no connection to steak. It's meant to be short for premium which is derived from a French word (Makes sense). A prime (prEEEEm) is an intermediate prize awarded within a race meant to encourage more aggressive competition during what may otherwise be a boring race. Primes are usually meaningless prizes, but riders will race their brains out for meaningless prizes.

Prologue: A short individual time trial before the first stage used to determine which rider will wear the leader's jersey. It's sort of a pre-stage or perhaps stage zero. I think it's derived from a French tradition.

Pulling or Taking the Pull: Being the lead rider in a paceline. Allowing other riders to draft. The principle is that the rider in front takes the majority of the wind resistance and the rider behind has to

GLOSSARY

work less to achieve the same speed. Smart riders find it wise to pull for only short periods of time. Even smarter riders find it wise to let someone else pull. See wheel sucker.

Quick release: The lever sticking out from the center of the wheel axle that allows the wheel to be removed without the need of wrenches. Make sure your quick release is snuggly in the closed position before any ride.

Rim: The outer part of the wheel that the spokes are attached to and the tire fits around.

Road rash: The skin that is removed when a rider crashes and slides along the pavement for a while. It's also known as a trophy and sometimes a biker's tattoo. Johnson and Johnson became very profitable from road rash.

Rookie Tattoo: The grease stain left on the right calf of the leg caused from the greasy chain ring. Rookies haven't learned to keep the chain ring off their legs yet.

Saddle: The apparatus on which the rider sits on a bicycle. It's a saddle, not a seat. It is properly referred to as a saddle. You probably have heard all of the crude jokes about saddles, so I won't elaborate.

SAG/SAG wagon: SAG stands for Support And Gear. They are support vehicles and crew that roam long rides and races providing assistance to riders in distress. Distress may include a mechanical problem, a medical problem, a fatigue problem or a follow-the-route-stupid problem. In extreme cases the SAG wagon will take riders who can't finish back to the start/finish area. SAG is good.

Schrader valve: An tire-tube air valve made like a standard car tire valve. These valves require a tire pump with an end that screws onto the valve so that all the air escapes when the pumper tries to unscrew the pump.

Seat post: The tube that protrudes from the *seat tube* that the saddle actually is attached to. The seat post is generally adjustable up and down. Okay; don't ask why it's a seat tube, but a saddle is not called a seat.

Seat Tube: The main frame tube between the bottom bracket and the top tube.

Skid Lid: Helmet. Early cycle helmets truly were brain buckets and often brain boilers. About the best they did was to keep the parts inside after a header. The early helmets provided little protection and often caused more harm than help.

GLOSSARY

Today's helmets are light, cool, and offer good head protection. (also see brain bucket)

Snake bite: A puncture that has two tiny holes relatively close together sometimes called pinch flats. These "snake-bite" flats may be caused by improperly installing the tube and allowing it to be pinched between the tire and the rim. Usually, though, they are caused by hitting a pothole or some other solid object with enough power to crush the tire into the rim thus causing a snake bite flat. Of course, actual snakes in Florida have been known to bite a tire.

Snickers: The perfect food for cyclists. Snickers contains the most essential food elements: chocolate, caramel and sugar with just enough peanuts to keep everything together. Snickers can be eaten before, during or after a ride. Snickers also are great incentive for your riding partners when carried in your jersey pocket. It acts like the old carrot-on-the-stick trick keeping a rider behind close to your wheel hoping to be able to grab your Snickers Bar. Don't worry about the chocolate mess on your hands; it'll wash off later.

Soigneur: (It's French, and I have no idea of its proper pronunciation. I just mumble it with a phony, nasal sound.) A supporting team crew member who does all sorts of behind-the-scene tasks in support of the riders. Often the soigneur is often the team masseuse as well.

Stage Race: A road race consisting of several individual races—stages—over several days. The rider with the least accumulated time is the winner.

Stage: One individual race within a stage race.

Trainer: A stationary cycling device allowing a rider to cycle while stationary. Some trainers are self contained cycling machines while others are designed so that a bike can be attached and ridden without moving. Trainers are used primarily so that a rider can simulate actual riding on those inclement weather days without going out into the rain or cold. I'm not sure which is worse, riding in the rain and cold or riding a trainer for three hours while your favorite football team loses.

Take a flyer: Ride away from the group. (See Off The Front)

Team: A group of riders racing in support of each other in order obtain a win for one of the group. Team members wear matching uniforms.

Technical course: A route or a race course that requires strong bike handling skills. Generally a

GLOSSARY

"technical course" involves lots of tight turns and bends and may include fast descents. Technical courses produce white knuckles, prayers, and occasionally road rash.

Time Trial: The race against the clock. This is a race where each rider is timed over a specific course. Riders are on the course alone with no assistance from fellow teammates. Riders leave a starting gate at regular intervals of, usually, one to three minutes. (see ITT and TTT)

TTT: Team Time Trial. In a TTT, teams ride against the clock together, but not in direct contact with other teams. Generally the team time is designated by fifth rider across the finish line. Drafting is essential to a successful TTT.

Top Tube: The main frame tube that goes from the head tube to the seat tube and runs roughly parallel to the ground. This is the tube that brings fear to the hearts of male riders.

Trackstand: The technique of balancing on the bike without actually moving forward. Trackstanding promotes road rash.

Tubular tires: Tubulars are bicycle tires that encompass the entire tube and are sewn together with the tube inside. They are often referred to as sew-ups. Tubulars are glued to a special, cupped wheel rim. Yes, I said glued, but they are glued with a really good, sticky glue. Tubulars make a wheel-tire combination that is much lighter and much more rigid than a clincher type tire. However tubulars, as you might guess, are not made for easy flat tire repair. Most riders don't even try to repair a punctured tubular. I know one cyclist quite well who attempted to repair tubular tires but eventually and quietly went back to using clinchers.

UCI: Union Cycliste Internationale or International Cycling Union. The UCI is the group that oversees international cycling competition. It is composed of a herd of old, grey-haired bureaucrats and fuddy-duddies who rule professional cycling with an iron walking cane.

USA Cycling: The governing body that oversees both sanctioned amateur and professional cycling competition in the United States. It is composed of a group of aging bureaucrats who aspire to be grey-haired bureaucrats at the UIC.

Velodrome: A cycling track or arena used for track racing. Velodromes are like stock car tracks for cycling.

Wall: A very steep climb.

GLOSSARY

Wheel Sucker: The lazy guy who is always drafting off someone's wheel and never takes the pull on the front.

Wheel Sucking: The technique of riding close to the rear wheel of another rider. In automobile racing it is called drafting. In everyday driving it's called tailgating. The principle is that the rider in front takes the majority of the wind resistance and the rider behind has to work less to achieve the same speed.

Yellow Jersey: The leader's jersey at The Tour De France. The yellow jersey has become a common term for a leader's jersey in stage races.

Yellow line rule: A ride/race rule in road cycling that states that riders may not cross over the center line in the road: "the yellow line." This seems like a common sense rule, but some riders need to be reminded. The chief official will remind riders that "the yellow line rule is in effect." Violating the yellow line rule may get a rider disqualified or turned into road kill.

CPSIA information can be obtained at www.ICGtesting.com
Printed in the USA
LVOW121939151112

307355LV00006B/37/P